Regional Unemployment and the Relocation of Workers

PRAEGER SPECIAL STUDIES IN
INTERNATIONAL ECONOMICS AND DEVELOPMENT

Regional Unemployment and the Relocation of Workers

THE EXPERIENCE OF WESTERN EUROPE, CANADA, AND THE UNITED STATES

Martin Schnitzer

PRAEGER PUBLISHERS
New York • Washington • London

The purpose of Praeger Special Studies is to make specialized research in U.S. and international economics and politics available to the academic, business, and government communities. For further information, write to the Special Projects Division, Praeger Publishers, Inc., 111 Fourth Avenue, New York, N.Y. 10003.

PRAEGER PUBLISHERS
111 Fourth Avenue, New York, N.Y. 10003, U.S.A.
5, Cromwell Place, London S.W.7, England

Published in the United States of America in 1970
by Praeger Publishers, Inc.

Library of Congress Catalog Card Number: 72-77004

Printed in the United States of America

PREFACE

In the Western countries a very high priority has been
assigned to the maintenance of full employment; fiscal and
monetary policies have generally been subverted to this end.
However, although low rates of unemployment have been maintained, particularly in the European countries, since the end
of the Second World War, regional unemployment at rates well
above national averages continues to be a problem. Although
efforts are made to attract capital into these regions through
the use of various government incentives, the fact remains
that many regions continue to remain unattractive because they
lack the necessary economic requisites to attract industry.
It is also apparent that fiscal and monetary policies can be used
to stimulate a high level of aggregate demand although their
impact is uneven among regions. An agricultural area, for
example, would be less likely than an industrial area, to be
affected by expansionary fiscal and monetary policies.

In addition to fiscal and monetary policies, the Western
countries, including the United States, have utilized employment or manpower policies which aim at increasing the mobility
and adaptability of their labor forces in the face of rapid
changes in technology. These policies are designed to affect
both the supply and demand sides of the labor market. They
cover the supply side in the development of skills, and the demand side in the creation of jobs for specific individuals,
groups, and locations. Prevention of job displacement, whether
from economic or technological causes, and the easing of adjustment when it occurs are the focus of employment policies.

One aspect of employment policy is the relocation of unemployed workers to areas where employment is available.
All Western countries, with the exception of the United States,
use relocation allowances to stimulate the geographical mobility of unemployed workers. The importance of these allowances in terms of cost and workers relocated varies from
country to country. In the United States, relocation assistance
has been used on an experimental basis under an amendment
to the provisions of the Manpower Development and Training
Act. A series of pilot projects in various states were designed
to assess how effective relocation allowances can be in increasing the mobility of unemployed workers. These projects,

v

which were recently completed, may lead to the adoption of a national program of relocation assistance for unemployed and low-income workers.

It is the premise of this study that a one-sided approach has been taken to the problem of regional unemployment. It has been assumed that the solution to this problem is simply to attract industry into a region through the use of tax incentives or other devices. A concomitant to this solution is the use of fiscal and monetary policies to keep aggregate demand at a high level. However, it can be pointed out that even though the national unemployment rate in the United States reached a low level of 3.2 percent in recent years, there were a number of counties with an unemployment rate in excess of 10 percent. From this, it would appear that a pragmatic solution would be to encourage workers in these counties to relocate in areas where employment is available. However, selection of those workers who are most likely to benefit from relocation is desirable.

This study presents an analysis of relocation programs as they have been used in Western Europe, Canada, and the United States. The author is indebted to Resources For The Future and the American Philosophical Society for providing grants which enabled him to examine these programs first-hand in all of the countries used in the study. The author is also indebted to the Joint Economic Committee of Congress, and Congressman Wright Patman, Chairman, for making the arrangements and appointments in Europe and Canada.

The author also wishes to acknowledge the assistance of Mr. Per Silenstam and Mr. Curt Canarp of the Swedish Labor Market Board; Mr. Duncan Campbell, Department of Manpower and Immigration, Ottawa; Mr. J. Jordan Watson, Labor Attache, British Embassy in Washington; Mr. Charles Davis, North Carolina Fund; Mr. Jack Matheny, West Virginia Department of Employment Security; Mr. Paul Corbin and Mrs. Audrey Freedman of the U. S. Department of Labor; and Dr. Charles Fairchild.

CONTENTS

LIST OF TABLES

Regional Unemployment and the Relocation of Workers

CHAPTER **1** GENERAL BACKGROUND
OF RELOCATION
PROGRAMS

INTRODUCTION

Regional differences in unemployment rates tend to be a
persistent phenomenon in all industrial countries because of
barriers to the geographical mobility of labor and capital in
the face of structural changes in the economy. General fiscal
and monetary measures aimed at stimulating aggregate demand have in some countries succeeded in causing general
inflation without seriously denting the problem of regional unemployment because a combination of factors--lack of mobility,
lack of skills, and age--serve to keep a number of people unemployed.

Attempts to rehabilitate a depressed area through the use
of subsidies to industry, and public works projects to improve
the infrastructure of the area, are going to be only partially
successful in solving the problem of unemployment. Such devices are of little use to some depressed areas whose economic
base has vanished. Also, the gains made by subsidizing the
location of industry in depressed areas must be balanced
against the losses suffered by the economy as a whole when
industry is induced to refrain from operating in other areas
where overall production costs are lower.

The purpose of this study is to examine the use of relocation assistance as a device to stimulate the geographic mobility
of unemployed and low-income workers. The premise of the
study is that there has been a one-sided solution as far as the
problem of depressed areas is concerned--to bring jobs into
the areas through the use of a wide variety of inducements to
industry--and that perhaps more consideration should be given
to moving unemployed, or underemployed, workers to areas
where employment is available. A balanced approach seems

more desirable, particularly when it is apparent that for one
reason or another some areas lack the resource base or are
isolated from the mainstream of economic activity.

In September, 1967, the National Advisory Commission
on Rural Poverty completed a year-long study of rural poverty
in the United States and submitted it to the White House. This
study reflected the public concern over poor rural environmental conditions, which have caused an exodus of thousands
of rural Americans--both Negro and white--to urban areas
throughout the United States. Usually lacking requisite job
skills, a number of these people have remained unemployed,
and countless others have gone on relief, thus compounding
already existing complex urban problems. This unprecedented
exodus is expected to continue.

Rural poverty is by no means a problem which is limited
to the United States. For example, rural-urban disparities
exist in Canada and are considered to be a matter of national
concern. In 1961, the rural non-farm family income in Canada
averaged 69 percent of the average urban family income, and
rural farm family income averaged 63 percent of average urban
family income. [1]

These disparities were compounded by variations which
existed between provinces. For example, in Nova Scotia,
average farm family income was $2,255 in 1961, an amount
which was less than half of the average urban family income
of $5,796 for the nation as a whole. Using two poverty income
criteria, total Canadian rural poor families in 1961 numbered
504,743 out of 1,158,107 rural families. (Poor rural non-farm
families were defined as those having incomes of less than
$3,000 a year, and poor rural farm families as those having
farms with a capital value of less than $25,000 and gross sales
of agricultural products of less than $3,750 a year.) Rural
poverty was most extensive in Newfoundland, where 68 percent
of rural families were classified as poor, compared with 44
percent for Canada as a whole and 22 percent for Ontario, the
most affluent province.

RELOCATION ALLOWANCES
AND LABOR MOBILITY

Government assistance in relocating low-income workers, or those who are unemployed and can find no prospect of employment in their home area, is a desirable yet conservative labor market policy. The idea was endorsed by President Nixon's task force on public welfare and presented to Secretary of Health, Education and Welfare Robert Finch as one of a number of recommendations in the area of poverty and welfare. The President's National Advisory Commission on Rural Poverty recommended that a relocation program be established on a national basis, to be administered by the Department of Labor, and that relocation allowances be provided for disadvantaged workers who cannot find gainful employment where they now live, but for whom jobs and training opportunities can be located in other labor market areas.[2] This recommendation is not at all inconsistent with other recommendations of the commission which aim at the improvement of employment opportunities in the rural areas.

Relocation assistance is the provision of financial assistance to help a worker move to an area where employment is available. It includes a payment of transportation cost to the new area of employment, the cost of removal of the worker's household goods, and a starting allowance to support the worker until he gets his first paycheck. Often a family allowance is included to support the worker's family until he gets his first paycheck.

There are several reasons for the use of relocation allowances to help unemployed or low-income workers move to areas where jobs are available:

1. In order to have a high rate of economic growth, there has to be a high degree of labor mobility. However, there is a bias against encouraging labor mobility as a method of dealing with regional unemployment. It is argued that it is easier to persuade industry to move to problem areas than it is to persuade the unemployed or the rural farm worker to move into a new environment. Financial inducements can get industry into a problem area, whereas the lack of mobility of the unemployed or low-income worker is not as easily overcome,

since the immobility stems from an innate unwillingness of
people to uproot themselves.

It can be argued, however, that some workers, when
given the choice between no work or part-time work in the
home area and full-time work in another area, will choose
the latter alternative. This has been demonstrated by the
success of certain labor mobility projects in the United States.

2.   High mobility of labor as well as of capital character-
izes the purely laissez-faire economy. Yet in the mixed
economies of today, government intervention is directed
toward the mobility of capital, leaving market forces to determine the mobility of labor. The assumption is that capital
needs the inducements to locate in a particular area, but labor
needs no particular inducement to leave the area.

This reasoning, when applied to the type of person relocation assistance is designed to help, is absolutely wrong. The
person who has been unemployed over a long period of time,
or is making an income of less than $3,000 a year, usually
does not have the financial resources to support a move to an
area where employment is available. He also is not aware of
job opportunities elsewhere. Lack of financial resources and
knowledge of existing employment opportunities are deterrents
to labor mobility.

3.   High rates of unemployment exist in certain areas
of the United States as well as in other industrial nations. To
reduce these rates, it is necessary to employ a number of
measures, since each measure by itself is likely to make only
a marginal dent in poverty and unemployment. Supported
movement of low-income or unemployed workers is a legitimate measure. If a worker can be induced to move from an
area where he can make $1,500 a year to an area where he
can make $3,500 a year, then the economy is better off. Even
if he returns to his home area, the chances are that he has
acquired some work habits that will improve his earning
capacity. The cost of the move to the taxpayers is not a total
loss.

4.   If the reduction of unemployment in less prosperous
regions is an important desideratum of economic policy--and
it is in most industrial countries--some of those who are out

of work could be expected to move, given suitable financial
inducements. Apart from the quick and direct reduction of
unemployment, such labor movement would simultaneously
alleviate labor shortages in rapidly expanding regions. Increased labor market efficiency would have some restraint
upon inflationary pressures which have built up in areas with
labor shortages. An excellent example of this point is the
situation of Stockholm, London, and other major European
cities where labor is in short supply and competition for
workers has driven up the level of wages as well as prices.
However, in other areas there are unemployed workers.
Movement of these workers to the cities can reduce the pressure on wages and prices.

Although this argument has merit, it is necessary to point
out that movement of workers from labor surplus to labor
shortage areas can also have a deleterious effect upon the latter in terms of housing and service costs. A common phenomenon in most major industrial cities in the United States and
Europe is a shortage of housing. An influx of workers com-
pounds this problem and adds to housing costs, as well as to
the cost of providing social services. In fact, if mobility of
the unemployed is to be induced, consideration has to be given
to the provision of housing in the demand, or labor-shortage,
area. It can be said that the major deterrent to a successful
relocation program is a lack of adequate housing in the demand
area. In Europe, where there is a chronic housing shortage,
there is opposition on the part of local residents to giving the
relocated workers any priority in housing.

In addition to the provision of housing, there are social
costs which have to be considered. These costs are to the
provision of welfare services, hospitals, schools, and other
forms of social capital. To a certain extent, a strain is im-
posed on these services by the influx of more people. Although
this strain can be alleviated through an expansion of the services, an increase in taxes is likely. However, the impact
on social services which would be caused by the induced immigration of unemployed workers can be controlled by limiting
the relocatees to a manageable number. It is also possible
to direct the flow of workers receiving relocation allowances
to areas where less strain will be put upon housing and social
services.

Assar Lindbeck, professor of economics at the University of Stockholm, in disagreeing with Swedish policies to attract industry into depressed areas, makes the following recommendations:[3]

1.   Avoid compensating, by means of subsidies, industries and localities which lack natural facilities for industrial activity. Also avoid compensating, by means of subsidies, localities which lack external economies.

2.   Let the structure of industry in the country follow the natural resources of the various parts of the country. Allow some regions to assume the character of forest areas, natural reserves, or recreational areas, if the comparative advantages for these regions are to be found in such areas.

3.   Make the greatest possible attempt to solve the unemployment problem in northern Sweden through moving the unemployed away from regions that lack the resources to attract industry. By all means, compensate labor generously for the inconvenience and costs associated with retraining and movement.

Lindbeck does not argue for the mass evacuation of depressed areas. He believes in limiting industrial location policy measures to areas with good development potential.[4] He realizes that measures to promote mobility of labor out of the depressed areas may not be effective in some cases. Nevertheless, he contends that not every depressed area must or should have industry to absorb the unemployed. He advocates a selective location policy which is aimed at the improvement of localities and areas with the greatest chance of being saved.

It is necessary to point out that movement of workers, particularly those with few or no skills, into large cities with acute housing shortages can compound the economic and social problems which exist. However, a rational labor mobility program would consider desirable alternatives, such as smaller cities which have employment opportunities.

Identified as a major ingredient in the current urban unrest in the United States is an accelerating pace of migration to the cities from the rural areas. It is estimated that between

500, 000 and 600, 000 persons are migrating to the cities from
the country each year. Legions of young people, many of whom,
are Negroes, and nearly all of whom are ill-prepared to cope
with urban life, flood into the cities. The net result is a continued decline of population in rural areas and the aggravation
of rural and big city problems. There is every evidence that
the growth of productivity in agriculture will continue over the
foreseeable future, and consequently the migration of people
from rural to urban areas will also continue.

It is argued that this exodus will continue from the rural
areas, compounding the current population imbalance, unless
steps are taken to prevent it. There is a need for putting new
factories in rural areas as well as providing better education
facilities for rural youth. This can be done through the provision of favorable credit to firms moving into rural areas,
improving the quality of available housing, developing quality
transportation facilities, upgrading the family farm, and building new rural-urban growth centers. A series of tax incentives
can also be used to encourage private investment in rural
areas. The incentives could include increasing the 7 percent
investment credit on machinery to 14 percent; providing a 7
percent investment credit on the cost of a building in which a
business was located; or allowing accelerated depreciation on
plant and equipment.

It is also argued that workers from certain types of areas--
mountain or rural--cannot stand the transition from a rural
to an urban type of living. If the worker leaves his home area,
to which he is tied culturally, he will soon return. It is pointless to try to relocate him; it would be better from a humani-
tarian standpoint to let him exist on welfare or provide him
with some make-work type of employment.

There is a considerable element of truth to the above argument. However, there is also a certain amount of defeatism
involved. If the worker subsists on welfare or make-work
employment, this can have a pervasive effect on his children.
Poverty will, in effect, continue to breed poverty. Difficulty
in adjusting to a new type of environment can be alleviated by
providing counseling and supportive services. Hopefully,
this would reduce the rate of return to the home area.

RELOCATION PROGRAMS IN
EUROPE

The European countries have maintained unemployment rates which have averaged 2 percent or lower during most of the postwar period.   Labor shortages have been endemic and inflationary pressures persistent.   Full employment has been the supreme economic goal, and unemployment levels generally equated with full employment in the United States would cause the demise of many governments in Europe.   This preoccupation with full employment stems from circumstances which prevailed in various European countries between the two world wars.   Unemployment rates were in general quite high during much of this period.   For example, the unemployment rate in Great Britain in 1921 was 17.8 percent; in 1922, 16.2 percent; and in 1923, 12.2 percent.   In 1932 the unemployment rate was 21.9 percent, and for the period 1933-37, the average annual unemployment rate was 14.2 percent.   In some regions of Great Britain, particularly in Wales, the unemployment rate was as high as 50 percent for the period 1930-39.   In Sweden, the average unemployment rate in the period 1923-30 was 11 percent; in the period 1930-33, the rate was 19 percent; and in the period 1933-37, the rate was 16 percent.   In the period 1929-39, the average unemployment rate was 16 percent.

It can be said that prior to the Second World War, the central economic problem in the Western capitalistic countries was unemployment.   It was thought that other problems would take care of themselves if this problem could be solved.   When postwar plans were laid in such countries as France and Great Britain, the main goal to be pursued was achieving full employment through government policy.   Governments in these and other European countries came to play a very important role in the process of maintaining a high level of employment. This role took two basic forms:

1.   Governments in Europe have entered into their economies as an important determinant of the total level of economic activity by developing and using appropriate fiscal and monetary measures that insure a level of aggregate demand adequate to absorb into use labor and other resources.   Keynesian economics has come to the fore, the basic idea being that full employment can be achieved through the use of

adjustments of a country's fiscal and monetary machinery.
Fiscal and monetary policies have been made subordinate to
the objective of full employment. Changes in taxation and
government spending have influenced output and employment.

2.   European governments also serve as a powerful force
in the determination of productive capacity. There is public
ownership of certain key industries, and there is also direct
participation. Government expenditures contribute to the
health, education, and training of the labor force, and hence
to productive capacity.

However, the use of fiscal and monetary policies to maintain a high level of aggregate demand and direct government
participation in increasing output should not be overemphasized
to the exclusion of active manpower policies, which the
European countries have also used as a part of full employment
policy. Manpower policies include not only the efficient allocation of labor resources, but also the social welfare of workers
themselves. Garth Mangum cites three goals of manpower
policies:[5]

1.   Employment opportunities for all who want them in
jobs which balance free occupational choice and adequate income with society's relative preferences for alternative goods
and services.

2.   Education and training capable of fully developing each
individual's productive potential.

3.   The matching of men and jobs, with a minimum of
lost income and production.

The latter goal is of particular relevance to the use of
relocation allowances. It is pointless to have unemployed
workers in one area and available jobs in another area. The
full and optimal utilization of resources is thus circumvented.
A viable manpower policy would include relocation allowances
in order to increase the efficiency of the labor market. In
several European countries the growth in the labor force has
been static. The postwar "baby boom," which became a permanent part of the U.S. scene, subsided quickly in Europe.
A labor shortage has developed and is expected to continue in
the 1970's. In such countries as Sweden and West Germany,

workers have had to be imported from other countries. It is estimated that close to 1, 000, 000 workers have been imported into West Germany from Yugoslavia, Greece, Turkey, and other countries.

Most European countries have had provisions for relocation allowances throughout the greater part of the postwar period. Great Britain has had a program for moving unemployed workers since the early part of the 1930's. In general, relocation allowances are a part of an overall manpower program which is administered by each country, and must be analyzed within this context. Budgetary appropriations are made for a variety of manpower measures, such as job training, unemployment compensation, relocation allowances, public works, and regional development grants. Although emphasis has been placed on the decentralization of industry and on policies which are designed to encourage industry to locate in areas where supplies of unemployed or underemployed workers may be found, relocation allowances are also provided to workers.

Eligibility for relocation allowances is confined to workers who are unemployed and are experiencing problems in finding employment in the home area. This eligibility is not necessarily limited to unemployed workers in depressed areas. More important is the inability of the worker to secure employment in the home area. In Sweden and Great Britain, however, workers who are likely to become unemployed also are eligible for relocation allowances. Reports of impending layoffs are usually given by firms to the Swedish employment service two months in advance. In France, relocation allowances are used as a device to get underemployed farm workers off the farms and into industry. In Canada, relocation of the unemployed is regarded as part of a program against poverty.

Canada also utilizes a program of relocation assistance. The problem of geographic distance is more acute than in the European countries, and almost any move on the part of a worker--unemployed or otherwise--would entail considerable cost. The problem of regional unemployment exists, particularly in the Atlantic region and portions of Quebec. To encourage relocation of unemployed workers, the Canadian government formerly provided loans and grants--the former for the short-term unemployed and the latter for the long-term unemployed. Now only grants are provided.

In Canada and the European countries, the expense of moving workers and the number of workers moved have been small relative to the total cost and number of workers affected by all employment programs. Nevertheless, national programs exist, and there is the underlying philosophy that when no employment is available in the home area, an unemployed worker should be assisted to move to an area where it is available. In several countries, the possibility of imminent unemployment is reason enough to support the movement of workers who would lose their jobs.

Relocation assistance has increased in importance in Great Britain and Sweden from the standpoint of financial outlays and the number of workers moved. In the National Economic Plan, which the Labor government adopted for Great Britain, relocation assistance was expanded as a matter of public policy to stimulate labor mobility and the rate of economic growth. France also has broadened its program by creating a national employment fund, which is designed to help workers adapt to structural changes in the economy.

Certain characteristics, which are relevant to the use of relocation assistance, are common to the economies of European countries as well as the United States.

1.   Although the unemployment rate in most of the countries is low by any standard, regional unemployment at a rate well above the national average exists. In the United Kingdom, for example, the unemployment rate in Northern Ireland is several times greater than the national average. The unemployment rate in Scotland is almost twice as high as the national average. In the United States, unemployment rates in some counties in Appalachia are two to three times the national average. In Sweden, two provinces in the northern part have had unemployment rates which were four times the national average.

2.   There has been a pronounced decline in employment in certain industries. The workers who are laid off often are unskilled and semi-skilled and are more difficult to absorb into other industries. Whole areas are affected by the decline

of an industry. In Sweden, there has been a decline in employment in the paper and pulp industry in the northern and central parts of the country. The textile and shipbuilding industries also have suffered declines in employment. Much of the unemployment in the United Kingdom has been in areas with declining industries. In Scotland, the problem is associated with a decline in employment in coal mining. In Northern Ireland, there has been a decline in shipbuilding. In Norway, there has been a decline in employment in the forest and fishing industries. In France, much unemployment has been associated with the textile and coal mining industries. Technological change in these industries will further accentuate the problem of regional unemployment.

3.   In several countries, notably France, there is a surplus of farm labor. With the attempt to achieve balanced economic growth throughout France, an effort is being made to get these workers off the land and into occupations that are in short supply. The same is true, to a lesser extent, in Sweden.

4.   In most countries, notably France and Great Britain, the problem of urban congestion has favored policies aimed at industrial decentralization. In France, a conscious attempt has been made to restrict further industrial development in the Paris area (roughly from Soissons to Orléans) by not subsidizing industry to relocate there. Subsidies of varying magnitudes are offered to industry to attract it to other areas, particularly to Normandy and Brittany. In London, control over building permits has the effect of forcing industries to other areas. The shortage of labor and space in the large metropolitan areas has brought about greater reliance on policies designed to encourage firms to locate in less industrialized and less congested areas.

5.   The lack of adequate housing in the larger cities appears to be a common denominator in most of the European countries used in the study. In Great Britain, lack of adequate housing is the major reason why workers receiving resettlement allowances return to the home area. The same problem exists in Sweden and France. The lack of housing probably has reduced by a considerable amount the number of workers who would utilize relocation assistance.

The public employment service in most countries handles
the administration of the relocation allowances. Usually, an
effort is made to find employment for the worker before he
leaves the home area. Once a position is found in another
area, the worker is referred to the employment office in that
area for placement. In many cases, job retraining precedes
the relocation of the worker. In Sweden, if the worker does
not have the requisite skills for employment in another area,
he is given job retraining in a center nearest the home area
and then assisted to move to an area where the job is available.

RELOCATION ASSISTANCE
IN THE UNITED STATES

A national program of relocation assistance for unemployed and low-income workers does not exist in the United
States. However, labor mobility pilot projects exist in a number of states, and are financed under funds provided under
provisions of the Manpower Development and Training Act
(MDTA). (The 1963 amendment to the Manpower Development
and Training Act included authorization for a program of labor
mobility demonstration projects. Section 208 authorized the
Secretary of Labor to carry out, in a limited number of geographical areas, pilot projects designed to assess or demonstrate the effectiveness in reducing unemployment of programs
to increase the mobility of unemployed workers by providing
assistance in meeting their relocation expenses.) Several
basic assumptions underlie the pilot projects:

1. High labor demand in one locality can often be
matched against excess labor supply in another area,

2. The financial cost of moving may often be a significant deterrent to the geographical mobility of unemployed
workers,

3. The benefits to society of providing relocation
assistance may more than compensate for the costs of such
assistance,

4.   The willingness to relocate, the feasibility of arranging relocation to unfilled jobs, and other aspects of any mobility assistance program may vary considerably by area and type of worker, so that exploration may indicate different values in different settings.

Demonstration projects sponsored under MDTA are designed to shed light on such assumptions. State employment security offices and private organizations in a number of states have conducted such projects. They seek to explore factors which affect the mobility of unemployed workers and their relationship to the availability of relocation assistance.

Several important questions must be answered in analyzing the success or lack of success of any relocation program:

1.   What factors stimulate or inhibit the geographical mobility of labor? In this connection, family ties, home ownership, lack of knowledge of existing job opportunities, and fear of the outside world would be factors that inhibit mobility.

2.   How many workers remain on the job once they have been relocated? This question is the most important of all. A high rate of return to the home area obviously will defeat the purpose of relocation assistance.

3.   How significant is financial assistance as a factor in promoting labor mobility? It is assumed that the type of person relocation assistance is designed to help would probably be insolvent because of an extended period of unemployment.

4.   What type of worker--unemployed or low-income-- can be moved through the use of relocation assistance? In general, it can be assumed that younger workers, with fewer family ties and a generally higher level of education, are easier to move than older workers.

5.   What problems--financial, social, or otherwise-- are met by relocated workers as a result of their moves? Relocation assistance is wasted if provisions are not made to smooth the transition of many workers from rural to urban environments. The adaptability of workers to a new and often

hostile environment is certainly a key determinant in the success or lack of success of a relocation program.

The labor mobility demonstration projects have not followed a set pattern. Some have concentrated on moving unemployed workers within state boundaries, while others have
moved unemployed workers to other states. Certain projects,
such as the North Carolina Fund labor mobility project, have
attempted to move low-income workers, i.e., members of
minority groups and tenant farmers, to areas where better
employment opportunities are available. Projects also have
used grants or loans, or both, to stimulate labor mobility.

SUMMARY

Full employment has become a desired public policy objective of major importance both in the United States and in
the countries of western Europe. The simplest definition of
full employment is an absence of involuntary unemployment.
The latter exists when workers are willing to work at pre-
vailing wages in their trade or occupation, but are unable to
obtain employment. However, in any country there are likely
to be varying amounts of frictional unemployment, which occurs whenever persons in the labor force are temporarily out
of work because of imperfections in the labor market. At any
given time, some workers will be in the process of changing
jobs or occupations. There are also likely to be varying
amounts of seasonal unemployment as some workers experience temporary lay-offs caused by the seasonal nature of their
work. Finally, there can be a certain amount of structural
unemployment, which is caused by shifts in demand that reduce the need for some types of workers and increase the
need for others.

Full employment policies involve the use of a government's
fiscal and monetary powers to influence the level of output and
employment. Fiscal policy embraces deliberate changes in
government expenditures and taxes as a means of controlling
the level of economic activity. The budget of the national
government is the key instrument through which fiscal policy
is effected. Fiscal policy therefore works through changes in

the budget, which, in turn, increase or decrease the level of spending in an economy. Monetary policy involves government control and regulation of the supply of money and credit. Control over the money supply will be reflected in changes in interest rates, which, in turn, will have an impact on spending.

It is necessary to differentiate between full employment policies and manpower policies. The former are quantitative in nature and involve changes in taxes, government spending, and the money supply to affect the general level of employment. The latter are qualitative in nature and involve changes in the composition and skills of the labor force. Manpower policies attempt to create jobs for specific individuals or groups, and to improve the skills of the labor force. They match the demand and supply sides of the labor market. With a concentration of unemployment among the unskilled and uneducated workers, it has become necessary to provide remedial measures to improve the quality of the labor force. Fiscal and monetary policies which are aimed at the maintenance of full employment must be complemented by a manpower policy which provides skills through education and training, and matches these skills to jobs through effective labor market programs.

Wide variations in income and employment exist within the regional framework of all major industrial countries. For example, average unemployment rates for the 50 U.S. states over a five-year period, 1958-62, ranged from 11.7 percent in West Virginia to 2.9 percent in North Dakota. [6] In 1969, Mingo County in West Virginia had an unemployment rate of 12 percent, while Montgomery County in Virginia had an unemployment rate of 1.9 percent--and the two counties are only 100 miles apart. [7] In Sweden, the unemployment rate ranged from 5.9 percent in the two northernmost provinces to 1.1 percent in Stockholm for the year 1967. Differences in incomes between states or between regions within a state also can be considerable. For example, in North Carolina, per capita income in 1966 ranged from $3,299 for Mecklenburg County to $1,156 in Gates County. [8]

Relocation assistance to move unemployed or low-income workers is an integral part of manpower policy. The rationale for its use is based on several factors:

1.   The financial cost of moving often can be a significant deterrent to the geographical mobility of unemployed workers. It can safely be assumed that most of the unemployed have few or no liquid assets with which to finance the cost of transportation.

2.   High labor demand in one locality can often be matched against excess labor supply in another area. Therefore, the benefits to society of moving the unemployed can more than offset the cost of their moving.

3.   Jobs cannot be brought to some depressed areas. Lucrative tax inducements and other concessions to attract industry can go only so far. It is significant to note that unemployment in certain areas of many countries continues to remain high despite attempts at area redevelopment.

NOTES

1.   Helen Buckley and Eva Tihanyi, Canadian Policies for Rural Adjustment (Economic Council of Canada, 1967) Special Study No. 7, pp. 27-28.

2.   President's National Advisory Commission on Rural Poverty, The People Left Behind (Washington, D.C.: U.S. Government Printing Office, 1967), p. 35.

3.   Assar Lindbeck, "Location Policy in Sweden," Skandinaviska Banken, Quarterly Review (June, 1964), 41-51.

4.   Ibid., p. 51.

5.   Garth Mangum, "The Development of Manpower Policy, 1961-65," in Sar A. Levitan and Irving H. Siegel, eds., Dimensions of Manpower Policy: Programs and Research (Baltimore: The John Hopkins Press, 1966), pp. 29, 30.

6.   Joseph M. Becker, ed., In Aid of the Unemployed (Baltimore: The John Hopkins Press, 1965), p. 39.

7.   Cited in The Roanoke Times (July 1, 1969), p. 17.

8.   Data compiled by the Agricultural Policy Institute, North Carolina State University, Raleigh, North Carolina (1969).

CHAPTER **2** SWEDEN

INTRODUCTION

Although Sweden is a small country, (173,423 square miles, the third largest country in Europe), with a population of around 8 million, it is one of the most advanced countries of the world in terms of living standards. It has the highest standard of living in Europe and is second only to the United States in per capita gross national product. The Swedish economic system is mixed, which means that there is both private and public ownership of industry. There is, however, little formal state ownership of industry, and in the Swedish economy, approximately 90 percent of what can be called the means of production is owned by private industry and individuals.

Probably the basic difference between Sweden and the United States lies in the all-inclusive social welfare program which covers each and every Swede from the cradle to the grave. In 1968, total social welfare expenditures amounted to 16 percent of the Swedish gross national product. The rationale for the social welfare program lies in a set of Swedish institutional factors which are different from those in the United States and, in the depression of the 1930's, probably caused a greater dislocation in the Swedish economy than was experienced in that of the United States.

The general economic policy of the Swedish government has been to achieve a high rate of employment. Monetary and fiscal policies have been subordinated to this objective. Throughout most of the postwar period, the Swedish economy has labored under inflationary pressures as the government has pursued a cheap money policy as an integral part of its full employment and social welfare programs. When a general decline in economic activity occurs, a series of employment measures are used, including emergency public works, extra government purchases from industry, and accelerated building construction.[1] These measures are a part of an active labor

market policy which has functioned in Sweden for some ten
years. This policy is an integral part of national economic
policy and is supposed to promote an adjustment between the
supply of and demand for labor, and provide selective measures
to increase employment without the overall effect of macro-
economic policy measures.

UNEMPLOYMENT

Sweden has had a very high level of employment since the
end of the Second World War. In fact, the supply of labor has
been so short that about 150,000 workers, mainly Finns and
and Norwegians, have been brought in. Unemployment has
averaged less than 2 percent since the end of the war. [2] However, there has been a downturn in employment during several
postwar recessions which also affected other western European
countries. It must be pointed out that unemployment during
these recessions was moderate by pre-war standards, reach-
ing a high of 4.3 percent in January, 1959.

Why, then, the concern with unemployment? There are
several reasons. First, seasonal unemployment has been
somewhat of a problem, ranging several points above the
average rate of 1.5 percent which has prevailed since the end
of the Second World War. Second, long-term structural
changes in several industries--textiles, forestry, clothing,
and shoe and leather -- have caused islands of unemployment
throughout Sweden. These structural changes have been in
part attributable to shifts in consumer demand and in part to
foreign competition. Third, upgrading of skills in response
to improved technology has resulted in the unemployment of
many semi-skilled and unskilled workers. Fourth, the export-
oriented economy has made Sweden vulnerable to a decline in
exports.

Seasonal unemployment has been a problem in northern
Sweden, particularly among the forestry workers. In January,
1962, the unemployment rate in Sweden was 2.1 percent; however, in the two northernmost provinces--Norbottens and
Vasterbottens--the unemployment rates were 6 and 6.3 percent, respectively. In February, 1965, the unemployment

rate for the two provinces was 5.9 percent, compared with
the national average of 1.7 percent. In February, 1967, the
provincial and national unemployment rates were 6.1 percent
and 2.1 percent, respectively.

The five northern provinces--Gavleborgs, Jamtlands,
Vasternorrlands, Vasterbottens, and Norbottens--contain
approximately 60 percent of the unemployed in Sweden. This
area, bordering on Norway and Finland, is far removed from
the centers of population, which are in central and southern
Sweden. Adverse climatic conditions (most of the land area
is north of the Arctic Circle) and an inadequate transportation
system make most of the area unattractive to industry. The
land area comprises half of Sweden, yet less than 20 percent
of the population lives there. Agriculture (represented largely
by small landowners), forestry, and mining account for 90
percent of the employment in these five provinces, and manpower requirements are decreasing in each of these industries.
The distances between industrial and commercial centers in
northern Sweden are much greater than in other parts of the
country, and these centers are, as a rule, fairly small. This
means that unemployed workers and new entrants into the
labor force find it particularly difficult to get jobs. The
Swedish Government owns, or has a controlling interest in,
a limited number of businesses, most of them set up or acquired in the public interest. The Norbottens Jarnverk (iron-
works) was built during the Second World War to increase
domestic steel production and also to create employment in
northern Sweden. The Statens Skogs Industries was created
from a number of private companies in the lumber, cellulose,
and paper industries to provide employment in a number of
localities in northern and central Sweden.

A migration from rural to urban areas has developed at
a steadily accelerated pace in Sweden. In 1930, less than
half of the population lived in urban areas, but by 1967, the
urban population had increased to 77 percent. This migration
is the result of structural changes which are taking place in
the Swedish economy. In 1930, agriculture and forestry employed 50 percent of the population of Sweden, but in 1967
only 10 percent. During the same period, industry increased
its share from 36 to 44 percent of the employment and the
service sector from 24 to 46 percent. During the 1960's,

structural changes have been taking place rapidly in the Swedish economy, particularly in the forest regions of northern Sweden.

A second problem area includes the provinces of Varm-lands and Kopparbergs. These provinces are in the western part of Sweden, bordering on Norway. The unemployment rate is considerably higher than the national average. The basic problem is a decline of employment in agriculture. In Varm-lands--a heavily forested province--three pulp mills, employ-ing 600 workers, closed recently. Most of the area of both provinces lacks the potential to attract industry.

Swedish employment policies recognize realistically that much of northern and central Sweden is inaccessible to trans-portation or lacks the resource base to attract industry. Sub-sidies to influence the location of industry in these area would, in the long run, be wasted. It is less costly and more prag-matic to induce the unemployed to leave by providing them with financial assistance to get to an area where employment is available.

THE NATIONAL LABOR
MARKET BOARD

The organization which is responsible for the entire em-ployment program in Sweden is the National Labor Market Board. In addition to operating a nationwide placement service, the board has the responsibility for putting into operation vari-ous employment-creating measures, such as the management of investment reserve funds, and for stimulating occupational and geographical mobility. Other responsibilities include the supervision of the public employment service, planning of projects suitable as emergency public works, direction of the start and discontinuance of such works, licensing of starting permits for building, and advice on location of new industrial establishments. The board functions as an independent agency under the Ministry of Interior Affairs.

The Labor Market Board is a tripartite board consisting of representatives from labor, management, and the govern-ment. There are two representatives from the Swedish

Employers' Confederation, two representatives from the Swedish Trade Union Confederation, one representative from the Central Organization of Salaried Workers, one representative from the Confederation of Professional Associations, one representative for female workers, one representative for agriculture, and three representatives from the government.

There are 25 county labor boards, 25 regional offices, and 233 local offices. They provide quick information on employment changes within their areas. County job vacancy lists are published by the county labor boards each week and are sent to the county employment offices. Vacancies which cannot be filled this way and which are suitable for exchange on the national level are reported by the regional employment office to the National Labor Market Board in Stockholm. In the Employment Service Division this material is compiled on a daily, as well as a weekly, basis for publication in national vacancy lists, which are distributed to all employment offices. Daily reports of vacancies filled are sent by the Employment Service Division to each office.

Information on job vacancies in different parts of the nation is broadcast daily over the radio. Advertisements in the newspapers are also used to inform the public on employment opportunities. Bulletins are read periodically on television, and folders are distributed in the employment offices.

Manpower Policies

Swedish manpower policies aim at increasing the mobility and adaptability of the labor force in the face of rapid changes in industrial development and at providing employment to workers who are displaced by technology or who are affected by seasonal lay-offs. These policy measures include relocation allowances and vocational training, public works, and tax incentives and grants. Unlike general monetary and fiscal measures for influencing the overall state of the economy, these measures are anti-inflationary with regard to cost and are selective with regard to the particular problem involved: the need to balance labor demand and labor supply in a country with an overall unemployment rate of less than 2 percent. Their functions can be described as an attempt to reduce the level of unemployment and satisfy the demand for labor by stimulating labor mobility between areas of oversupply and areas of excess demand.

Public works are an important means of reducing seasonal unemployment, especially in northern Sweden, where this type of unemployment is high among forestry and agricultural workers. This device is also used to even out cyclical fluctuations in employment. It involves the construction and maintenance of roads, the repair of bridges and channel facilities, the preparation of firebreaks, and other projects which can be completed in a short period of time.

Investments in public works are the responsibility of the Labor Market Board and are made out of funds which are made available for employment stabilization purposes from the national budget. Public works are started when unemployment cannot be alleviated by relocation allowances and job retraining The extent and scope of public works are dependent upon general economic conditions and the type of unemployment.

In addition to public works, there are special projects for handicapped workers, including the mentally retarded. These workers are given vocational training and placed in sheltered workshops which are supported in part by production orders from Swedish industry. Other handicapped workers, including older workers whose skills have become obsolete, are given employment in centers for relief work which have been created in most Swedish counties.

Government grants and loans to attract industry into problem areas have been available since 1965. This aid is intended primarily for the development of the northern provinces, but may be extended to other parts of the country where problems of unemployment exist or are expected to occur in the immediate future. It takes the form of subsidies to support the cost of constructing a building and installing equipment. (Grants or loans to firms locating in depressed areas can amount to 50 percent of the cost of building and equipment.) Swedish enterprises also are allowed to draw on their investment reserve funds, provided they are used for investment in plants and equipment in depressed areas.

Perhaps the best-known manpower policy, one which has received worldwide attention, is the Swedish investment reserve. It is a device, incorporated in the Swedish tax structure, which is designed to help iron out economic fluctuations by encouraging private corporate savings in periods of high profits and private capital expenditures in periods of unemployment. Swedish companies are encouraged to set aside a part of their pre-tax profits in a reserve; and if these funds are disbursed for investments in buildings, machinery, and inventories during a period when investment is desirable, substantial tax privileges are attainable.

The investment reserve works as follows: Companies are permitted to set aside, at their own discretion, up to 40 percent of pre-tax income as an investment reserve for economic stabilization. This amount is deductible from income for the purpose of the national and local corporate income taxes, which amount to a combined total of 49 percent of net income. Forty-six percent of the reserve must be deposited in a non-interest-bearing account in the Central Bank of Sweden, and the remaining 54 percent becomes a part of a company's working capital. No government permission is needed to set aside this reserve. However, control over the use of the reserve is exercised by the Labor Market Board. [3]

The investment reserve law was enacted in 1938. The basic intent of the legislation creating the reserve was the provision of a tax device which, by permitting postponement of taxation, would enable companies to build up reserves for use as a source of investment, and hence employment, in the event of a depression. However, it has been put to practical use as an instrument of fiscal policy only in the past 10 years.

Another employment-creating device used in Sweden is an increase in national and local governmental purchases from industry. Orders are placed and financed either by the Labor Market Board on behalf of the governmental units for which the purchases are intended, or by the units themselves after consultation with the Labor Market Board. Funds can come from two sources: (1) an increase in the regular state appropriations for this purpose and (2) special funds which are made available to the Labor Market Board. Purchases from industry may be made at the onset of a recession or when a given industry lacks sufficient orders to maintain its personnel. For example, in

January and February, 1968, public orders for machinery were increased to forestall a decline in employment caused by a reduction in exports. The Labor Market Board also obtained the government's permission to extend to counties and municipalities subsidies covering 20 percent of the orders for machinery and equipment placed by them over and above their previously established purchasing programs.

Measures which are designed to promote occupational and geographic mobility are also the responsibility of the Labor Market Board. Changes in the occupational structure and in the geographical distribution of available work often lead to discrepancies between the qualifications of the available labor and the qualifications currently in demand. Old trades die out or have to be supplemented by training in new methods. Entirely new jobs develop, and the qualifications necessary to fill them must be acquired. A shortage of skilled labor can prevent industries from entering expanding market situations.

Job training in Sweden is used for solving the employment problems of certain categories of workers: unemployed or underemployed workers (particularly in labor surplus areas), disabled persons, job seekers who are difficult to place because of their age, and seasonally or temporarily unemployed workers. However, training is not necessarily limited to these categories, but is available to workers in general. Rationalization processes within manufacturing industries have created the need to upgrade skill requirements for many occupations. Training grants, which are paid for a period of up to two years, are available for the worker who undergoes job retraining. They include a training allowance of 550 kronor a month ($105) for a married person and 500 kronor a month ($95) for a single person, a rental allowance which ranges from 85 kronor ($16) to 125 kronor ($20) a month, and a family allowance of 150 kronor ($28) a month for the spouse and 60 kronor ($11) a month for each child under 16. However, the rental and family allowances are payable only if the training takes place away from home.

In 1967, 70,000 persons received job training in Sweden, and in 1968 the total was 76,000. This was out of a total labor force of 3.2 million persons. Thus, approximately 3 percent of the Swedish labor force received some type of job training in these years. Since the U.S. labor force is approximately

24 times the size of the Swedish labor force, this would mean
that in comparable terms, some 2 million American workers
would receive government-supported job training. However,
this is not the case. Job training in the United States lags
well behind training in Sweden in terms of numbers and financial support.

Coupled with job training are measures designed to promote
the geographical mobility of labor. Unemployed workers and
workers who are faced with imminent unemployment receive
relocation allowances to assist their movement to areas where
employment is available. Geographical mobility is considered
necessary for an effective manpower policy. By using selective measures, such as relocation assistance, the Labor
Market Board tries to facilitate a balance between labor supply
and demand.

Table 1 presents the total cost of Swedish manpower policies for the fiscal year 1968-69. The significant point to be
remembered is that these expenditures represent a commitment on the part of the Swedish government to the maintenance
of full employment.

This total of 1.7 billion kronor ($330 million) represented
a budgetary outlay of about 1.2 percent of the Swedish gross
national product for 1968. Translated into U.S. terms, equivalent expenditures on U.S. manpower policies would have had
to have been $8.5 billion for the fiscal year 1968-69. This
amount is more than the budget for the U.S. Department of
Labor for the same fiscal year. The gross national product
of Sweden for 1968 was 142 billion kronor ($26 billion), and
the gross national product of the United States for the same
year was $860.7 billion. This means that Sweden allocates
a much larger amount of its gross national product to expenditures on manpower policies than does the United States.

Total labor market expenditures by the Labor Market
Board are set at 2.1 billion kronor, out of the Swedish draft
budget of 42 billion kronor for the fiscal year 1969-70. Expenditures on manpower policies account for approximately 5
percent of total budgetary expenditures of the national government. Although not the largest expense item in the appropriations from the budget for labor market policy, retraining measures and the relocation of manpower are considered to be the

TABLE 1

Appropriations for Swedish Manpower Policies, Fiscal 1968-69

Title of Appropriation	Amount in Thousand Kronor (1 krona = about $.19)
Labor Market Board, administrative costs	25,170
Employment exchanges, administrative costs	117,130
Public works	415,000
Special relief work	320,000
Temporary accommodations	22,700
Retraining and relocation	350,000
Regional development grants and loans	210,000
Cash assistance to the unemployed	175,000
Miscellaneous	70,101
	1,705,101

Source: National Labor Market Board.

most important components of labor market policy. Expenditures in the period 1960-69 on retraining measures increased
from 25.1 million kronor to 320 million kronor, and expenditures on relocation allowances increased from 5.8 million
kronor to 59 million kronor. The recession of 1967, with the
highest unemployment rates of the decade, and continued structural changes in the economy have contributed to these expenditure increases.

Forecasting

As a rule, twice a year the Labor Market Board collects
from the county labor boards surveys on the expected developments in the labor market in each county, one covering the
summer and the other the winter. The prediction of the expected development is based on comprehensive statistics from
enterprises typical of the various trades in the industry of
each county. This information is gathered through question-
naires and interviews with the heads of firms. It includes
data on the amount of incoming orders, volume of production,
inventories, market prospects, planned investment in buildings
and machines, unfilled vacancies, and expected lay-offs or
increases in personnel.

Systematic and comprehensive manpower forecasting is
of recent origin in Sweden. However, a special section of the
Vocational Guidance Division of the Labor Market Board, called
the Forecasting Institute, is responsible for long-term employment forecasts. These forecasts form the basis for long-
term employment policy as well as for vocational guidance.[4]
Demand and supply forecasts by occupation and industry are
currently being made. Structural changes which can be expected in the composition of the labor force are also being
examined.

Advanced Warning of Lay-offs

A system of advance information on impending employment
changes is used in Sweden. It is based on agreements between
the Labor Market Board and different employers' associations.

Anticipated discharges of labor have to be reported by a company to the county labor board, usually two months in advance. The same is true for governmental organizations. This information, gathered from county and local offices all over Sweden, is reported to the Labor Market Board in Stockholm.

When reporting to the county labor board, a company states (1) the date when the expected discharge or lay-off is likely to be put into effect, (2) the number of workers expected to be discharged, (3) the estimated duration of the unemployment, and (4) the reasons for the curtailment of production.

RELOCATION ASSISTANCE

Sweden considers the use of relocation assistance to be an important part of its overall employment and manpower policies. This use dates back to 1912, when unemployed workers could obtain public funds, in the form of a loan, to cover the cost of travel to an area where employment was available. In 1932, the loan was transformed into a grant. This assistance was originally regarded as an unemployment measure and was based on a means test. In 1958, the use of relocation assistance became a formal part of Swedish labor market policy and was used to promote manpower adjustments in the labor market. The travel grant was broadened considerably, and the use of the means test was eliminated. Family, removal, and special installation allowances were incorporated into the relocation assistance program. Government financial support has increased considerably since 1958, and today the program is the most extensive in the world. There are two reasons for the increase in this support:

1. Relocation assistance contributes to a better balance between different sub-markets within the total labor market,

2. It is the responsibility of the government, in certain circumstances, to assume responsibility for the cost of moving unemployed workers from areas where there are no employment opportunities to areas where jobs are available.

The use of relocation assistance as an employment device is of more importance in Sweden than in any other country included in this study. The percentage of workers moving with such assistance is considerably higher than in other countries, and the percentage of government expenditures on relocation assistance relative to other employment-creating measures also is higher. The probable reasons for its importance in Sweden are a willingness on the part of the government to experiment with a wide range of employment measures and a lesser degree of political interference from the problem-area representatives to the Riksdag than one might expect. Relocation assistance to unemployed workers also has had the support of labor and management.

Although Sweden has had considerable success with its relocation program, it should be pointed out that there are four factors which help to make for its success.

1.   The homogeneity of the population is an important factor. The Swedes who move from northern Sweden to Stockholm or Goteborg will encounter other Swedes who possess the same social characteristics. It is also to be noted that 99 percent of the population is Lutheran, and there are no significant racial minorities. However, some Swedes from the forest areas of the north and from the rural areas in general have not found city living compatible with their former way of life, and have left employment in the cities for the more insecure employment in their home area.

2.   High levels of employment exist throughout most of Sweden. A general labor shortage has existed in the industrial areas since the end of the Second World War. This means that jobs are available for the unemployed in the depressed areas. It is only a matter of inducing them to leave. This is done through the use of relocation allowances.

3.   The presence of a first-rate employment service. The employment offices throughout Sweden know of all job vacancies. The unemployed worker is notified of existing vacancies in other areas. It now becomes merely a matter of matching the worker with the vacancy.

4.   If the worker lacks the requisite skills to secure employment, vocational training is provided. In Sweden, vocational training plays a paramount role in employment policy. Training courses are scheduled by the Labor Market Board and administered by the Central Board for Vocational Training. The number of courses offered has increased from 55 in 1957 to 822 in 1968. Instruction is given in some 80 different specialized occupations, with periods of training varying from one month to two years.

The relocation allowances take four forms: travel allowances, family allowances, starting allowances, and settlement allowances.

Travel Allowances

Travel allowances include the cost of travel expenses, subsistence while traveling, and expenses for the removal of furniture and other possessions. The total allowance may be paid either in the form of a grant without liability for repayment or as a loan with a liability for repayment. The latter is not common. Arrangements for this allowance are made through the employment office in the worker's home area.

1.   Travel expenses--These expenses are payable for the following purposes:

(a) Journeys to seek employment or to take employment at another place. A worker who is declared eligible for travel allowances by the local employment office can receive travel expenses to look for a job. He is under no obligation to take the job if it is offered to him. In fact, he can return home and look for another job with the assistance of another travel grant. The merit of this arrangement is that the worker is not compelled to take the first job that becomes available.

(b) A return trip to the worker's home, provided that through no fault of his own the job never began or was discontinued a short time after his arrival.

(c) Daily journeys, for a period of not more than three months, when the worker has to remain at his original home and commute to work until he is able to find housing.

(d) A return trip to the place of prospective employment if his employment is to begin at a later date.

The amount of the travel allowance depends upon the mode of transportation. If the journey is made by public conveyance, the allowance must not exceed the cost of the cheapest mode of transport. If the worker uses his own car, compensation is based on an amount equivalent to the cheapest fare by public conveyance for the distance covered.

2. Subsistence expenses--An allowance for board and lodging is payable to a worker for expenses incurred in transit while looking for a job. A day allowance (25 kronor) is payable when a journey is made between 6 a.m. and 12 midnight, and a night allowance (15 kronor) when the journey takes place between 12 midnight and 6 a.m.

This subsistence allowance is also payable when the worker is moving to a new job. His wife and children between the ages of four and 18 are also eligible for an allowance.

3. Removal allowances--A travel allowance is payable for the removal of a worker's family and household furniture to the new employment locale. Payment is made for the expenses of the personal transportation--which would include the cost of transporting the family from the old to the new locale, freight charges for moving the worker's furniture, and the expenses of packing, unpacking, and handling of furniture.

Family Allowances

The Labor Market Board may pay family allowances in cases in which the worker is to take employment in a new place where he cannot immediately find family housing. This allowance is to compensate the family for the expense of having to maintain two separate residences.

The family allowance is granted for a period not to exceed one year, and is exempt from income tax. For the first six months, the allowance is not more than an amount equivalent to the actual rent, including heating costs, for the family in the home district, plus a supplementary living allowance. For the next six months, not more than one-half of the amount above is payable.

This allowance is payable up to the time when housing can be found in or near the new place of employment. The amount of the allowance is as follows:

For the first six months, a supplementary family allowance for the wife of 450 kronor a month, a supplementary family allowance for children under 16 at a rate of 60 kronor per child per month, and a housing allowance, including heating costs, which is not to exceed 300 kronor a month, For the second six months, the amount payable is reduced by one-half.

Starting Allowances

This allowance is granted to cover the worker's living costs until the first payday. The amount of the starting allowance depends upon the estimated duration of employment. It begins at 250 kronor if the estimated duration of employment is under two months and increases by 250 kronor for each two months, to a maximum of 1,000 kronor if the duration of employment is more than six months.

The starting allowance is payable by the county labor market board in the county where the place of employment is situated. The board in the new place of employment has to check after 30, 60, and 90 days to see whether the employment is still in effect.

There is an obligation to refund the starting allowance, at the rate of five kronor a day, if the worker terminates the new employment without good reason. For example, a worker receives an allowance of 150 kronor. He works 25 days and then decides to return to his home. He would have to refund 125 kronor. If, however, the worker moves to another job during the first six-month period, he is not liable for repayment,

provided his change of employment is considered suitable
from the labor market point of view.

Settlement Allowances

Settlement allowances are a special form of relocation
allowance which are paid to unemployed workers who move
from areas with particularly high and persistent levels of unemployment (northern Sweden only) to other areas of the country. They amount to a lump-sum payment of up to 2,000
kronor for the worker and 150 kronor for each child under 16.
The idea behind this special allowance is that the unemployed
from northern Sweden are so far behind the rest of the population that it is necessary to give them a new start in life, so
to speak. This settlement allowance will enable them to get
new furniture and clothes and will help them adjust more
readily to the new environment.

Still more has been done to stimulate labor mobility. A
deterrent to labor mobility is the ownership of a home and the
reluctance to take a loss if it has declined in value. Since the
decline in value is a fact in many depressed areas, in 1964
the Swedish Riksdag passed legislation to compensate homeowners in northern Sweden for any loss in the market value
of their homes. A homeowner is paid the difference between
the appraised value of his home and the selling price. Compensation was paid to 168 homeowners during the period from
July, 1964, to July, 1968. The total cost of compensation
was 3 million kronor ($580,000), approximately $3,500 per
home.

Eligibility Requirements

To be eligible for the various relocation allowances, a
worker must meet the following requirements:

1. The worker must be unemployed or, in the opinion
of the employment service, likely to be unemployed in the
near future.

2.   It must be the judgment of the employment service
that the worker cannot be offered employment in the near future
at or near his place of residence.

3.   The new job cannot be regarded as a transfer between jobs within the same firm.

4.   The worker will take up employment at another
place, and the labor market situation in the new place is judged
by the local employment office to be such that manpower from
another area is required to fill the vacancy in question.

5.   The worker must live in a labor surplus area.

Cost of the Program

An idea of the cost of the Swedish relocation allowance
program can be obtained from Table 2.

The total cost of the program has increased considerably
since the fiscal year 1958-59. Particularly sharp increases
were registered during the fiscal years 1963-64 and 1967-68.
These increases were in part attributable to improvements in
relocation allowances and in part to an increase in unemployment which occurred during both time periods. A rough ap-
proximation of the cost of the Swedish relocation program if
applied to the United States--assuming similar allowances--
would be $144 million. The labor force of the United States
is 24 times as great as Sweden's.

The number of unemployed workers involved in the relocation programs is presented in Table 3.

In Sweden, as in most industrialized countries, there is
a shortage of housing in the areas of the country with expanding
industry and a demand for labor. This housing shortage has
complicated the leveling between areas with a labor shortage
and those with a surplus. Different measures have been used
to overcome this obstacle to the mobility of labor.

More than 90 percent of housing construction in Sweden
is supported by government loans. When these loans are

TABLE 2

Cost of Relocation Allowances, by Types, 1958-68
(thousand kronor)

Fiscal Year (July 1-June 30)	Starting Allowances	Family Allowances	Travel Allowances	Settlement Allowances	Total
1958-59	600	2,252	416	-	3,328
1959-60	2,102	2,761	915	-	5,778
1960-61	1,993	2,492	1,148	-	5,633
1961-62	2,292	2,224	1,575	-	6,091
1962-63	3,400	2,814	2,912	623	9,750
1963-64	9,538	4,557	6,071	3,336	23,502
1964-65	9,744	5,020	7,632	4,096	26,490
1965-66	8,432	4,245	6,556	3,122	22,355
1966-67	7,476	5,207	5,441	3,013	21,137
1967-68	9,866	7,943	9,829	3,580	31,218

Source: National Labor Market Board.

TABLE 3

Number of Persons Receiving Relocation Allowances, 1958-68

Fiscal Year (July 1-June 30)	Starting Allowances	Family Allowances	Travel Allowances	Settlement Allowances	Total
1958-59	2,200	1,881	3,212	-	7,293
1959-60	8,164	2,110	7,465	-	17,739
1960-61	7,898	2,116	9,850	-	19,864
1961-62	8,725	2,068	12,000	-	22,793
1962-63	12,895	2,678	20,124	220	35,917
1963-64	22,290	3,769	38,000	1,780	55,839
1964-65	22,120	3,112	39,422	2,072	66,726
1965-66	20,589	2,649	35,564	1,680	60,482
1966-67	15,871	2,797	32,613	1,344	52,625
1967-68	22,498	4,332	47,133	1,673	75,636

Note: An individual can get more than one travel allowance, so the actual number of individuals receiving travel allowances is less than the figures indicate. The same is true for starting and family allowances, because it is likely that some persons changed jobs during this period and received the allowances again.

Source: National Labor Market Board.

granted, special account is taken of the demand for housing in and around areas with expanding industries. Extra loans are placed at the disposal of these areas, on the condition that priority in housing is given to the unemployed from labor surplus areas. The National Labor Market Board also can build temporary houses for workers where there is a great demand for labor.

The great majority of workers receiving relocation assistance lived in the northern and central provinces of Sweden. Table 4 presents a breakdown of relocation allowances by provinces.

The importing, or receiving, areas for the workers receiving relocation allowances are presented in Table 5. The two major importing areas were--as might be expected--Stockholm and Stockholm Province. Much migration to the cities of Goteborg and Malmo has also occurred. Considerable migration has taken place within several of the problem regions. In the province of Varmlands, many of the unemployed were absorbed in industry which has developed around Lake Malaren. In Norbottens and Vasterbottens, movement has been from the forest and farming areas to communities which have succeeded in attracting industry.

The age breakdown of the workers receiving relocation allowances revealed no significant characteristics which would differentiate the group from workers in general. About 46 percent of those workers who received starting allowances were less than 22 years of age. Approximately 22 percent were over 35 years of age. It is apparent that the older workers are attached to their home areas and prefer to work on public works projects in the winter and eke out a marginal existence in the forests in the summer. A complaint with respect to the public works program in northern Sweden is that it prevents many of the marginally employed workers from migrating to other parts of Sweden where full-time employment is available. This is particularly true for the older Swede. Although age discrimination supposedly does not exist in Sweden, it can be assumed that employment priority is given to the younger worker.

TABLE 4

Number of Persons Receiving
Relocation Allowances, by Province, 1964

Province	Starting Allowances	Family Allowances	Settlement Allowances	Total
Varrmland	1,356	273	-	1,629
Kopparbergs	1,781	398	60	2,239
Gavleborgs	2,161	387	182	2,730
Vasternorrlands	2,969	467	466	3,902
Jamtlands	2,356	346	293	2,995
Vasterbottens	3,155	414	431	4,000
Norbottens	4,986	710	720	6,416
Total	18,764	2,995	2,152	23,911
Total for Sweden	23,194	3,662	2,152	29,008

Note: These figures are for the complete year (January-December) rather than the fiscal year, which runs from July 1 to June 30. This is why the totals do not match those in Table 3 which were based on fiscal year totals.

Source: National Labor Market Board.

40

TABLE 5

Major Receiving or Importing Provinces for Workers Receiving
Relocation Allowances, 1964

Receiving Area	Number
Stockholm (city)	2,982
Stockholm (province)	2,649
Uppsala	850
Malmohus[1]	1,080
Goteborgs och Bohus[2]	1,361
Vastmanlands	1,634
Gavleborgs	1,215
Norbottens	1,135
Total	12,906
Total for Sweden	23,194

Note: The data cover the calendar year 1964.

[1]The large industrial and seaport city of Malmo is located in this province.

[2]Goteberg, the second largest city in Sweden, is located in this province.

Source: National Labor Market Board.

TABLE 6

Distribution of Starting Allowances by Age and Sex, 1964

Age	Male	Female	Total Number	Total Percent
Under 18	1,935	2,015	3,950	17.0
18 to 21	4,399	2,269	6,668	28.7
22 to 24	2,297	576	2,873	12.4
25 to 34	3,853	458	4,311	18.6
35 to 44	2,641	249	2,890	12.5
45 to 54	1,789	185	1,974	8.5
55 to 59	365	19	384	1.7
60 to 66	131	13	144	0.6
Total	17,410	5,784	23,194	100.0

Note: The starting allowance is the best measure of the actual number of workers who received relocation assistance, for it, is paid to all workers--single or married--when they take new employment. Assuming that a small minority of the 23,194 workers changed jobs more than once during 1964, it is probable that around 22,000 workers were actually moved under the Swedish relocation assistance program.

Source: National Labor Market Board.

Results of the Program

The success of these measures to stimulate geographical mobility is unquestionable. For instance, according to Bertil Olsson, Director General of the National Labor Market Board, "It costs less than 1 million kronor to move 1,000 persons to employment. For the same amount, these persons might have been given unemployment assistance for less than two months or employed on public relief works for not more than five days. . . ." The measures have been made selective, with the intention of reducing pools of unemployment by removing workers to jobs elsewhere. The measures have been expanded since 1957, when the stimulation of geographic mobility became an important part of the overall employment program. In 1958, the family allowance was introduced, and one year later, the starting allowance was instituted. In 1962, the settlement grant became a mobility measure, and in 1964, compensation to homeowners for a decline in the market values of their homes was introduced.

However, a legitimate question is whether the workers remain in their new jobs after the government has subsidized their movement, or whether they return to their home area. Several investigations have been made in an attempt to answer this question. One study embraces the period from January, 1963, to March 1, 1964.[5] Under observation were those workers who received a starting allowance in January, 1963. The number of workers included in the investigation amounted to 1,091. About 80 percent of the allowances went to workers in the five northern provinces of Sweden and the provinces of Varmlands and Kopparbergs. These workers took up employment in the provinces around Lake Malaren, Stockholm, Malmo, and areas in southern Sweden. Half of the men and four-fifths of the women were under 25 years of age.

By the end of February, 1964, the following information was obtained:

Still in original job for which they received
    starting allowances   415
In other employment   411
Unemployed   52

Employed on public works   17
Military service   44
Married and withdrew from labor market, or
    pregnant   36
Job training programs   39
Miscellaneous   77

Although the majority of all workers who had received starting help in January, 1963, had left the original job by the end of February, 1964, it cannot be deduced that the Swedish government had spent a considerable amount of money to relocate these workers in vain. A sizeable number (411) had moved to another job, usually in the same area as the initial job. (Forty-seven received the starting allowance for a second time.) Some had withdrawn from the labor force and others were in military service. Only 52, 5 percent of the total, were unemployed at the end of the period involved in the study. Some workers returned to their home community or province when employment became available.

The results of this study are presented in Table 7, which indicates the duration in initial employment for the 1,091 workers receiving starting allowances.

Lack of adequate housing, although not as pronounced a problem as in Great Britain, is a factor which has caused some workers to leave their jobs. The Labor Market Board, however, has provided temporary housing for some workers in areas where there is a great demand for labor.

The use of relocation assistance is one part of an overall Swedish employment policy aimed at maintaining full employment. Its importance relative to other employment measures is hard to determine. Although a cost comparison of various employment measures can be made, one cannot conclude that one measure is more important than another because of the costs involved. A program of public works obviously will cost more than a program to relocate unemployed workers, but that does not mean that the benefits derived are proportional to the costs.

An idea of the cost of various Swedish employment programs can be obtained from Table 8.

TABLE 7

Age Distribution of Workers Receiving Starting Allowances, by
Length of Employment

| Age | Left employment after these months | | | | | Still employed in March, 1964 | Total |
	1	1 to 3	3 to 6	6 to 9	9 to 12		
Under 18	7	20	29	9	9	30	104
18 to 21	40	55	83	28	22	111	339
22 to 24	5	27	37	8	12	71	160
25 to 34	23	42	51	15	14	105	250
35 to 44	9	25	31	10	3	60	138
45 and over	6	17	25	3	6	38	100

Source: Undersokning Rorande Personer Som Starthjalp, Arbetsmarknadsstatistik, No. 11 B
(Stockholm: National Labor Market Board, 1964), p. 11.

45

TABLE 8

Estimated Expenditures on Employment Policy Measures, 1964-65

(in kronor)

Relocation measures

Travel allowances	4,500,000
Family allowances	7,000,000
Starting allowances	7,500,000
Temporary housing	3,500,000
Total	22,500,000

Public relief measures

Work on roads and streets	250,000,000
Other relief work	70,000,000
Work in archives	21,000,000
Aid to industry	6,500,000
Other measures	7,000,000
Total	354,500,000

Source: Statsverksproposition ar 1964, Bil. 13, Inrikesdepartementet, p. 85.

Approximately 6 percent of the total estimated cost of Swedish employment policy measures amounted to (22, 500, 000 kronor) was allocated to relocation of the unemployed. This was an increase over fiscal 1962-63, when relocation allowances amounted to 10, 600, 000 kronor[6] out of 398 million kronor spent on all employment measures--about 2. 5 percent.

A comparison of the cost of subsidizing the location of industry in problem areas with the cost of moving the unemployed out of the areas can also be made. Table 9 presents a comparison of costs to attract industry with costs of relocating unemployed workers. The seven provinces with the highest unemployment rates are used. It is necessary to point out that there is some migration of the unemployed within the seven provinces. The data presented are for different time periods, but a rough comparison can still be made of the two approaches.

When the cost of relocation assistance is compared with the total cost of the overall labor market program, the proportion is small. For example, for the fiscal year 1968-69, appropriations for relocation assistance amounted to 52 million kronor ($10 million) out of a total budgetary appropriation to the Royal Labor Market Board of 1. 7 billion kronor ($320 million). However, the importance of relocation assistance in comparison with the other employment measures is difficult to determine, for it is impossible to conclude that one employment measure is more important than another because of the costs involved. Also, the matter of geographic distance is of less importance in Sweden than in the United States, because Sweden is not much larger than the state of California.

In 1968, 21, 744 Swedes, out of a total labor force of 3. 2 million, received travel allowances to take up employment in a new location. The average unemployment rate in Sweden for 1968 was 2. 1 percent. This means that, on the average, some 65, 000 persons were unemployed. In terms of the movement of the unemployed, it can be said that travel allowances to take employment were of considerable importance. Although it is difficult to make comparisons between Sweden and the United States, it can be estimated that if travel allowances had been used on the same scale in the United States, some 450, 000 persons would have received them. This estimate is based on the ratio of 24 to 1 between the labor force in the

TABLE 9

Comparison of Costs of Government Subsidies to Attract
Industry to Depressed Areas and
to Relocate Unemployed Workers, 1964-65

(in kronor)

Province	Government subsidies to attract industry [1]	Government subsidies to relocate the unemployed [2]
Varmlands	4, 715, 000	1, 560, 000
Kopparbergs	6, 600, 000	1, 890, 000
Gavleborgs	5, 888, 000	2, 430, 000
Vasternorrlands	12, 499, 500	3, 510, 000
Jamtlands	6, 771, 300	2, 700, 000
Vasterbottens	7, 798, 600	3, 510, 000
Norbottens	11, 834, 000	5, 670, 000
Total	56, 106, 400	23, 270, 000

[1] July 1, 1964 - March 31, 1965.
[2] Based on author's estimates. The estimates were obtained by taking the average amount of each type of allowance and multiplying by the number of workers receiving each type of allowance in each province. The figures are based on all allowances given during 1964.

Source: National Labor Market Board; author's estimates, based on National Labor Market Board and other information, including Arbetsmarknadspolitik 1965, pp. 116-129.

48

United States and Sweden. Actually, the average unemploy-
ment rate in the United States was considerably higher than
in Sweden--about 3.6 percent. This means that approximately
2.8 million persons were unemployed, on the average, in 1968.
The ratio of travel allowances to the number of unemployed in
Sweden is 1 to 3. If this ratio were applicable to the United
States, it would mean that some 900,000 unemployed workers
would have received travel allowances to secure employment.
This is approximately 100 times the actual number in the
United States who were moved under various experimental
programs.

On an a priori basis it might be argued that Americans
are more mobile than Swedes and do not need relocation allowances to induce mobility. However, the facts do not bear this
out. The Swedes are a much more homogeneous people who
live in a much smaller country. There are no regions isolated
from the rest of the country by geographical barriers, and no
areas of poverty. In fact, Sweden is a highly industrialized
country with a standard of living second to that of the United
States.

SUMMARY

The prime desideratum of post-war economic policy in
Sweden has been the maintenance of full employment. To accomplish this objective, the Swedish government has chosen
to use not only general measures of economic policy, but also
special means of stimulating employment, the latter usually
described as labor market or manpower policy. Although
Swedish employment policies have been successful on a national
basis, unemployment rates have been much higher in certain
parts of the country than in others. Accordingly, labor market
policy has attempted to increase the mobility of the labor force.
The aim has been to transfer manpower from districts and
industries suffering from unemployment to those with a grow-
ing need for labor. This is accomplished through reliance on
job retraining and relocation allowances.

Relocation allowances are of four types: travel allowances,
family allowances, starting allowances, and settlement

allowances. They are provided for workers who are unemployed and cannot find employment in their home districts. Workers who are seasonally unemployed, or who are in imminent danger of becoming unemployed, are also eligible for relocation allowances. Most workers who receive relocation allowances are from the forest provinces of northern Sweden, where considerable unemployment exists. The number of individuals receiving relocation allowances has increased tenfold during the ten-year period July, 1958, to June, 1968. Expenditures increased sharply in the fiscal year 1967-68, reflecting a recession that started in the fall of 1966.

In the future, the conditions upon which relocation allowances will be given are to be broadened. For example, farmers who possess small land holdings and who need a supplementary job to maintain an adequate standard of living are to be given relocation grants and retraining if they change occupation. Relocation allowances are also to become supplements to retraining for occupations in which there is a labor shortage.

Regional unemployment is a problem which confronts Sweden and other industrial nations. Even though national unemployment rates are low, considerable variations exist between regions, and are expected to continue in the future. Sweden has used a balanced approach to this problem. Investment grants and other inducements are given to firms to locate in areas with above-average unemployment rates. However, this approach alone is insufficient, because there are some areas that lack the economic base to attract industry or are too isolated from urban market centers. Thus, relocation allowances play an important role in overall Swedish policies to maintain a high rate of employment. Unemployed workers are moved at state expense to areas of the country where jobs are available. The number is large relative to the total number of persons who are unemployed during a given period of time, and would be even larger were it not for a shortage of housing in the major Swedish industrial cities.

NOTES

1.   See Martin Schnitzer, "Unemployment Programs in Sweden," Joint Economic Committee Monograph, Congress of the United States (Washington, D. C. : Government Printing Office, 1965).

2.   For the measurement of unemployment in Sweden, see President's Committee to Appraise Employment and Unemployment Statistics, "Measuring Employment and Unemployment," pp. 250-251.

3.   For comprehensive analysis of the Swedish investment reserve, see Martin Schnitzer, "The Swedish Investment Reserve," American Enterprise Institute Monograph, (Washington, D. C. : 1967).

4.   For a comprehensive description of the long-term forecasting procedure in Sweden, see Sten Olof Doos, "Long-Term Employment Forecasting--Some Problems with Special Reference to Current Organization and Methods in Sweden," in pp. 29-69 of an overall report on employment forecasting by Jan Tinbergen, Director of the Netherlands Economic Institute, Rotterdam. This report concerns forecasting procedures which are currently being used in France, the Netherlands, and Sweden.

5.   "Undersokning Rorande Personer Som Erholl Starthjalp, 1 Januari, 1963," Utgiven av Kungl. Arbetsmarknadsstyrelsen, No. 118 (1964).

6.   Statsverkspropositionen ar 1964, Bil. 13, Inrikesdepartementet, p. 85.

CHAPTER **3** GREAT BRITAIN

INTRODUCTION

Regional unemployment is a problem in Great Britain, where for many years there have been considerable differences in prosperity between regions. In the northern and western parts of the country, unemployment and net emigration have been higher, and per capita income and the rate of economic growth lower, than in the Midlands and the southern part of the country. The uneven distribution of unemployment has been a political problem for a number of years.

The economic record of Great Britain throughout most of the period since 1948 shows highly favorable employment conditions combined with a rather low rate of economic growth and considerable instability. From 1948 to 1960 the national unemployment rate averaged about 1.5 percent. (British unemployment statistics are based on a count of unemployed registrants at employment exchanges and youth employment offices. Registrants include persons seeking unemployment benefits, unemployed workers who are not eligible for benefits but who wish to apply for national assistance grants, and those who are not eligible for either benefits or grants but wish to use the services of the employment exchanges. In terms of the American system, the British unemployment rate is understated by about 0.8 percent.)[1] Even in the recession year of 1958, unemployment rose only slightly above 2 percent. During the period from 1960 to 1965, the national unemployment rate averaged 1.6 percent. However, the austerity measures of the Wilson government, which were designed to correct an imbalance in the nation's balance of payments, caused the unemployment rate to rise above 2.6 percent in 1968.

Heavy emphasis has been given in Great Britain to a high and stable rate of employment, and lesser emphasis to price stability and economic growth. Extensive use of tax devices was made after the Second World War to influence both the level and the composition of economic activity. Monetary policy also was subverted to this end. The rationale for the pursuit of policies which were aimed at the maintenance of full employment is easy to understand. In the decade prior to the Second World War, the average rate of unemployment in Great Britain was over 10 percent. In some areas of Scotland and Wales, the average rate was 20 percent or above. The White Paper on Employment Policy, issued by the coalition government in May, 1944, set out the policies to be pursued after the war to maintain full employment. To achieve this objective, certain industries were nationalized, including the Bank of England.

Government relocation assistance to unemployed workers moving to take jobs in new areas has been available for more than 30 years. During the depression, there were relocation schemes for which the legislative authority was contained in unemployment insurance legislation. However, the massive unemployment that existed in Great Britain during the depression made the use of relocation allowances of little value. In the White Paper on Employment Policy, a program of relocation assistance was recommended as a part of a viable national employment policy. Formal support for a national program of relocation assistance was given by Sir William Beveridge, who probably had more influence on postwar economic policy in Great Britain than any other person. In his book, Full Employment in a Free Society, he writes as follows:[2]

... action against unemployment must be taken on three lines - of maintaining at all times adequate total outlay; of controlling the location of industry; of securing the organized mobility of labor. The first of these is the main attack; the others are subsidiary - mopping up operations. Employment depends on outlay, that is to say on the spending of money on the products of industry; when employment falls off, this means that someone is spending less; when employment increases, this means that in total more is being spent...

Beveridge felt that if there was a demand for labor at fair wages, men who were unemployed for any substantial period of time should be prepared to take employment and not hold out for work in their own place. However, it was up to the Labor Exchanges to find them employment and to pay for the cost of their relocation.

UNEMPLOYMENT IN GREAT BRITAIN

British economic policy over the last 20 years, if judged solely in terms of the objective of maintaining a high level of employment and disregarded from the standpoint of in- flation and an unfavorable balance of payments, has been very successful. Unemployment expressed as a percentage of the total number of workers in Great Britain, has not ex- ceeded 3 percent. However, some regions have had an un- employment rate which has been consistently higher than the national average. These regions include Scotland, northern England, and Wales. Problems exist in these regions and in Northern Ireland which seem to resist all attempts to make an appreciable reduction in the unemployment rate. Lucrative inducements to industry to set up operations in these regions have at best stabilized the rate of unemployment.

The unemployment rate in Scotland and the northern region has always been consistently higher than that for Great Britain in general. Table 10 affords an interesting comparison:

However, differences in unemployment between counties and districts in Great Britain have been even more pronounced, particularly during the depression of the 1930's. For example, in Scotland in 1935 the unemployment rate for Ayrshire was 21.1 percent, 7.1 percent for the district of Dalmellington, and 50.8 percent for the district of Kilwinnig. Both districts are within the county. In Wales in 1935 the unemployment rate for Caernarvonshire was 19.4 percent. The district of Llanberis had an unemployment rate of 5.2 percent and the district of Caernarvon had an unemployment rate of 33.3 per- cent. Glamorganshire had an unemployment rate of 36.4 per- cent, and the districts of Resolven and Ferndale had unem- ployment rates of 10.7 percent and 67.6 percent, respectively.

TABLE 10

Unemployment Rates in Scotland, Northern England,
and Great Britain, Selected Periods
(percent)

Period	Scotland	Northern England	Great Britain
1923-27	13.8	15.2	10.9
1930-34	24.4	27.5	19.0
1938-39	14.9	17.7	10.3
1948-52	3.0	2.4	1.6
1960-62	3.6	3.4	1.7

Source: British White Paper No. 2188, An Inquiry into the Scottish Economy, p. 44; no. 2206, The North East, A Program for Regional Development and Growth, p. 43.

In England, Lancashire had an unemployment rate of 20.5 percent in 1935, while the districts of Leyland and Hindley had unemployment rates of 5.1 percent and 40.8 percent, respectively.

There are in general four problem regions in Great Britain: Scotland, Northern Ireland, Wales, and northern England. This does not mean, however, that all of Scotland or all of Wales can be considered a problem region. It means that there are areas within these two regions that have above-average unemployment and below-average incomes. These areas are usually dependent upon coal mining or shipbuilding, which have declined in importance in recent years.

Scotland

The Toothill Report on Scotland states: "For half a century high unemployment and persistent emigration, coupled with slow overall economic and population growth have been features of the Scottish economy."[3]

Unemployment since the end of the Second World War has persisted at twice the national average. Even an outmigration of 375,000 persons from 1951 to 1964 failed to have any appreciable effect on unemployment. During this same period of time, the number of employed males in the labor force decreased by 33,000, while there was a national increase in male employment of one million. Historically, Scotland's industrial structure was based on the primary and heavy capital goods industries which in the last decades have faced shrinking world and home markets. There has been a continuing loss of employment in coal mining, shipbuilding, marine engineering, and metal manufacturing. Employment in the primary industries--agriculture, forestry, fishing, and quarrying--also continues to decline. In 1963, 20.4 percent of Scottish workers were employed in manufacturing industries that were expanding in terms of employment and output, while 17.6 percent were employed in industries that were contracting. This can be compared with 33.2 percent and 3.7 percent, respectively, for the West Midland region of Great Britain.

From 1959 to 1962, there was a decline in employment of
26, 300 in the primary industries and 32, 000 in such manufacturing industries as those mentioned above.   This decline
of 58, 300 was offset by a gain in employment of 62, 000 in the
service industries and 47, 900 in such industries as electronics,
electrical engineering, and machine tools.   However, cross
mobility from coal mining and shipbuilding to services and
electronics is uncommon.

Northern Ireland

Northern Ireland may be considered as the major problem
area of the United Kingdom.   It has consistently had the highest
rate of unemployment of any region, and per capita income is
15 percent below the national average.   From 1953 to 1963
the unemployment rate in Northern Ireland was more than
four times the rate for Great Britain--7. 5 percent versus
1. 7 percent.   In March, 1965, the unemployment rate for
Northern Ireland was 6. 8 percent, compared with 1. 6 percent
for Great Britain.   In March, 1967, the respective unemployment rates were 6. 9 percent and 1. 9 percent.   In 1963, 18. 2
percent of Northern Irish workers were employed in manufacturing industries that were expanding in terms of employment and output, while 27. 5 percent were employed in industries that were contracting.   These percentages can be
compared with the averages for Great Britain: 28. 6 percent
and 11 percent, respectively.

An increase in employment in new manufacturing industries, the service trades, and construction has been more
than offset by a contraction of employment in the older industries, shipbuilding and linen, and agriculture.   Shipbuilding has presented a particular problem.   Belfast, which
for many years was one of the leading shipbuilding centers in
the world, has lost out to shipbuilding centers in Japan and
other countries.   In 1965, the closing of one of the major
shipyards in Belfast resulted in the loss of 7, 000 jobs.   Despite emigration, unemployment has remained persistently
high in Northern Ireland, and has rarely been below 5 percent since the Second World War.   A high rate of natural increase has ensured an overall increase in the population,
further compounding the problem of unemployment.

The Northern Region

The northern region of England includes Northumberland, Durham, and the North Riding of Yorkshire. It also has been consistently an area of unemployment except for the period 1951-57, when the unemployment rate approached the national average. Since 1957 the unemployment rate has averaged about 50 percent above the national average. The region depends heavily on a few basic industries--coal mining, shipbuilding and marine engineering, iron and steel manufacturing, and heavy engineering. Employment in these industries either has been declining or has stopped rising, partly because of rationalization and technological advances which are in themselves a sign of industrial health. Coal mining, the major industry in the region, employed 16 percent of the total male work force in 1963. However, much of the coal production is uneconomical, pits are closing, and employment is dropping sharply. Many miners have been moved to more profitable coal mines in northern Staffordshire and elsewhere through the use of relocation allowances granted by the National Coal Board.

Wales

The unemployment rate in Wales is a little less than twice the national average. It is higher than in the northern region and only a little lower than in Scotland. Northeast Wales, in particular, has persistently been a problem area. Coal mining and agricultural employment have declined sharply since the end of the Second World War. In mid-Wales, an extensive and largely mountainous area, there has long been a problem of unemployment, economic decay, and dependence upon state grants and subsidies. Additional problems of the Welsh economy are a decline in railroad employment and the relative inaccessibility of many parts of Wales to the rest of Great Britain.

In October, 1967, the unemployment rate in the northern region of England was 4.1 percent, compared with an unemployment rate of 1.6 percent in London and the Southeast. The unemployment rates in Scotland and Wales were 3.8 and 4.0

TABLE 11

Unemployment Rates for Great Britain and Selected
Regions, 1963-68

Unemployment Rate

Year	Great Britain	Northern Region	Wales	Scotland	Northern Ireland	London and Southeast
1963	2.5%	5.0%	3.7%	4.8%	8.0%	1.5%
1964	1.6	3.4	2.6	3.7	6.6	1.0
1965	1.4	2.6	2.6	3.0	6.1	0.9
1966	1.5	2.6	2.9	2.9	6.1	0.9
1967	2.4	4.0	4.1	3.9	7.7	1.6
1968	2.4	4.6	4.0	3.8	7.2	1.6

Source: Department of Employment and Productivity, London, April 1969, pp. 80-83.

percent, compared with a national average of 2.4 percent and an average of 1.9 percent for regions with low unemployment.

Unemployment rates from 1963 through 1968 showed little change in the pattern that had prevailed for several decades. In general, the combined unemployment rates for the problem areas of Great Britain have remained, on the average, twice as high as in the country as a whole. An implication that can be read into Table 11 is that while general increases in aggregate demand created a high level of employment in Great Britain as a whole, unemployment remained at about twice the national level in the northern region, Scotland, and Wales, and four times the national level in Northern Ireland.

These rates, however, do not reveal differences in unemployment within these regions. For example, the unemployment rate in Northern Ireland in April, 1969, was 7.1 percent. In the area of Ballymena, the unemployment rate was 2.7 percent; and in Londonderry, it was 12.7 percent. In Belfast, the unemployment rate was 5.6 percent, compared with a rate of 14.9 percent for Newry. Unemployment rates for Wales and Scotland in April, 1969, were 4.5 percent and 3.9 percent, respectively; unemployment rates within Wales ranged from 2.1 percent for Shotton to 7.4 percent for Bargoed, and unemployment rates within Scotland ranged from 2.5 percent for Aberdeen to 7.8 percent in the Highlands. [4]

THE RELOCATION OF WORKERS

Before proceeding to an analysis of worker relocation schemes in Great Britain, it is necessary to examine the country's geography and population. The land area of Great Britain is approximately 88,700 square miles. England, the largest component, contains 50,300 square miles; Wales, 8,000 square miles; and Scotland, 30,400 square miles. The population of Great Britain is approximately 52 million. Northern Ireland has a land area of 5,500 square miles and a population of 1.5 million. The density of population in

Great Britain is one of the highest in the world, exceeded only
by Japan, Belgium, and the Netherlands among major industrial countries. This density has caused considerable
problems in the major cities, and is a factor which has played
a major role in national economic policy decisions. Population
shifts have resulted in a degree of regional imbalance. London
and southeastern England, in particular, have become over-
crowded with respect to the rest of Great Britain. If the proposed tunnel which is to connect Great Britain to continental
Europe is ever completed, more pressure will be placed on
London and southern England in terms of population density
and industrial development.

The problem of regional unemployment has been viewed
as a serious one since the end of the Second World War, and
it has occupied the attention of both Labor and Conservative
governments. However, this attention has not been disposed
toward impartiality between the alternative methods of equal-
izing regional differences in unemployment: movement of
labor out of regions of high unemployment into regions where
labor is needed, or the movement of capital in the reverse
direction. On the contrary, there has been little disposition
toward the placement of equal reliance on incentives to stimulate the geographic mobility of labor; in fact, problem areas
are favored by tax allowances to encourage the location of
industry, special aids for training to provide local employment, and cash grants to stimulate investment. Industrial
location is also influenced by government direction of private
investment through a system of industrial development certificates. Regional employment premiums also are paid to
manufacturing firms in the problem areas in order to encourage
an increase in the employment of labor.

Problem areas in Great Britain are called development
areas. There are five such areas: southwestern England
(Exeter, Plymouth, and contiguous areas), Merseyside
(Liverpool and areas on the Mersey River), the northern
region, Scotland, and Wales. The unemployment rate in
these development areas was 4. 2 percent in April, 1969. A
number of financial inducements are available to firms that
locate or expand in these areas. In fact, it can be said that
labor market policies in Great Britain are based primarily
upon the use of location subsidies which are designed to provide

employment for workers in the development areas. The major location subsidies are as follows:

1. Investment grants are made available for capital expenditures on new machinery or equipment installed for use in Great Britain by manufacturing, construction, and extractive industries. The rate of the grant is 25 percent; the purpose of the grant is to stimulate the development of the capital-intensive industries of Great Britain in order to increase the rate of economic growth. In development areas, the rate of the grant is 45 percent. In Northern Ireland, which has a development program of its own, the rate is 50 percent.

2. Another subsidy which is unique, by international as well as British standards, is the Regional Employment Premium. Its purpose is to subsidize employment in the development areas. Benefits are 30 shillings ($3.60) a week per full-time male manufacturing employee, 15 shillings ($1.80) per female employee, 15 shillings for boys, and 9 shillings 6 pence for girls. [5] This subsidy is justified as an export incentive as well as a contribution to a reduction in regional unemployment rates. Service industries are excluded from the premium.

3. The British government also can make capital grants toward the cost of constructing a factory in a development area. These grants amount to 25 percent of the cost of the plant and, in special cases, 35 percent will be given.

There has been a massive infusion of cash grants and other financial aids to firms locating or expanding in the development areas. For example, it is estimated that the cost of employment premiums alone is £100 million ($240 million) a year. If employment premiums were used in the United States on a similar scale, the cost would be at least $1 billion a year. These financial distributions are often a strong factor in altering location advantages. It is also necessary to remember that in a country the size of Great Britain, distances to markets are no problem. It is possible for firms to locate in a development area and be within 100 miles of a major metropolitan market area, such as Birmingham or London.

It is also important to remember that population pressures have created a serious problem in many areas of Great
Britain. It can be said that aid to industry in the development areas constitutes a form of holding action in terms of
keeping the population with them. Although a reduction in the
total number of unemployed workers could be accomplished by
the transfer of some of these workers from labor surplus
areas to areas of excess demand, particularly in the South
and Midlands, where two-thirds of the employed population
work, housing and public service considerations have to be
considered.

In spite of continual and increasing efforts by the British
government to decrease the disparity between the high- and
low-unemployment areas, there does not seem to be any trend
toward equality. (See Table 11.) In fact, changes in the national unemployment rate are associated with wider changes
in unemployment in the development areas.

Three separate programs for moving unemployed workers
to jobs exist in Great Britain. These programs are administered by the Ministry of Labor, the National Coal Board, and
the British Railways System. There is also a separate program which is administered by the government of Northern
Ireland.

Although coal and railroads are nationalized industries,
their relocation programs are considered to be employer
programs, since they are financed out of receipts of the industries. [10] Unemployed workers in the coal and railroad
relocation programs are moved within the industries. A
coal miner who becomes unemployed in a mine in Scotland
can transfer to another mine where employment is available.
Since a considerable reduction in employment has occurred
in coal mining and railroading, it has made sense to com-
partmentalize relocation programs under the agencies directly responsible for the administration of these industries.

There are three separate programs which are administered by the Ministry of Labor.

The Resettlement Transfer Scheme

This program is designed primarily to assist unemployed
workers with poor employment prospects in their home areas
to move to jobs in other areas, to resettle permanently or
to remain until work may be available nearer their homes.
The current program has been in existence since 1948, when
the Employment and Training Act[6] was passed. The actual
relocation of unemployed workers is carried out under this
scheme. Workers who are expected to be redundant also
are eligible for assistance.

Key Workers Scheme

This program is intended to assist employed workers who
are transferred either permanently or temporarily beyond
daily traveling distance of their homes in order to hold key
posts in plants which their employers are setting up in development districts.[7] Transfers must be approved by the Ministry
of Labor. However, it must be demonstrated that workers
of the same type cannot be found in the development area.
This transfer scheme is limited to workers who earn £1,500
or less.

The Nucleus Labor Force Scheme

This scheme assists firms that are setting up new factories in areas of high unemployment to recruit unemployed
workers living in those areas and to transfer them temporarily to parent factories for training. On completion of
training, and when the new factories are ready for occupation, the workers are returned to the home area to form a
trained nucleus labor force ready to start the new factories
into production. All training arrangements must be approved
by the Ministry of Labor.

During transfer, certain of the provisions of the Resettlement Transfer Scheme are available, for a maximum
of two years from the date training starts.

Eligibility

The Resettlement Transfer Scheme applies to the following types of unemployed:

1.   Those who have no early prospect of obtaining regular employment in the home area;

2.   Those who transfer beyond daily traveling distance of their homes to employment in new areas;

3.   Those whose transfer has the approval of an employment exchange as suitable for assistance under the scheme;

4.   Those who are not entitled to similar allowances from their employers.

The scheme also applies to those who are expected to become redundant (i. e. , to be laid off in the immediate future).   The scheme is not limited to depressed areas.

A person who qualifies for grants and allowances is, six months from the date of transfer, required to decide whether he wishes to remain in the new area or to return to the home area as soon as suitable work is provided for him.

Relocation Assistance Available

All transferred workers, whether they have dependents or not, are entitled to fare for the journey to take up employment in the new area, fares for the worker or his dependents in emergencies, and a settling-in grant of £5.

Transferred persons who continue to maintain dependents in the old home can receive the following:

1.   Lodging allowance--to assist a worker to meet the additional cost of living away from home, a contribution toward the cost of lodging will be paid at the rate of 70 shillings (about $8. 40) a week for a period of up to two years.

2.   Assisted fares for visits home--if the worker is entitled to receive a lodging allowance, he is eligible to receive assistance toward the cost of fares to visit his home. He is expected to pay the first 12 shillings, 6 pence of the fare. Six assisted fares are available during a year.

3.   Continuing liability allowance--if the worker's dependents join him in the new area and he is still liable for rent, mortgage interest, etc., for a house or apartment in the old area, the lodging allowance will cease but a continuing liability allowance up to a maximum of 70 shillings a week will be paid.

Additional allowances available to workers who decide to resettle permanently in the new area with their dependents are the following:

1.   Household removal assistance--payments will be made for the approved cost of the removal of furniture and personal effects of an ordinary private household, subject to the prior approval of the estimate by the employment exchange.

2.   Incidental expenses--a grant of £30 will be paid toward incidental expenses on completion of the household's removal to unfurnished accommodations.

3.   Dependents' fares--a free travel warrant will be issued to enable the dependents to join the worker in the new area.

4.   Sale and purchase of a house--a transferred worker who sells his house in the home area and/or buys a house in the resettlement area will receive a grant not exceeding £120 toward three-quarters of the cost of the solicitor's and house agent's fees incurred in transactions which are completed within two years of the date of transfer.

Results

As stated previously, employment policy in Great Britain is aimed at taking jobs to the workers rather than workers to the jobs. Provisions introduced under the Industrial Development Act of 1966 make it attractive for industries to locate in the development areas, where unemployment is higher than the national average.

A comparison of the two approaches underscores the above point. From the passage of the Local Employment Act of 1960 to the end of 1964, the British Board of Trade offered assistance to industries to the amount of £101 million. Relocation schemes cost the Ministry of Labor approximately £ 700, 000. [8]

The total costs and the number of workers moved under the Ministry of Labor's worker relocation program is presented in Tables 12 and 13.

The increase in the cost can be attributed to an increase in benefits in 1965 and an upswing in unemployment which began in late 1966. The total cost in 1968 was $1.2 million. If the relocation schemes were transferred to the United States, the cost would be very difficult to estimate, but a minimum of $10 million would do as a guess. The distances involved in travel would be much greater in the United States, and the total number of unemployed workers would be five times greater than in Great Britain.

The number of workers moved under the Resettlement Transfer, Key Workers, and Nucleus Labor Force schemes is presented in Table 13. The number of workers relocated is minuscule compared with the size of the British labor force (20 million) and the number of unemployed (in April, 1969, 561, 000).

Fewer than 5, 000 workers have been moved under the relocation programs of the Ministry of Labor in any given year. This number can be compared with a total regional migration in Great Britain of some 700, 000 workers a year. However, there are certain factors which have to be considered. First of all, there are other relocation programs,

TABLE 12

Cost of Relocation Programs of the Ministry of Labor, 1962-68

Financial Year[1]	Cost
1962-63	£110,121
1963-64	240,808
1964-65	175,577
1965-66	366,479
1966-67	381,817
1967-68	500,595
April-December 1968	421,413

[1] April 1 - March 31.

Source: Department of Employment & Productivity, Ministry of Labor (May, 1969).

68

TABLE 13

Number of Workers Moved Under Ministry of Labor
Relocation Schemes, 1962-68

Financial Year	Resettlement Transfer Scheme	Key Workers Scheme	Nucleus Labor Force Scheme
1962-63	2,722	89	16
1963-64	3,864	115	22
1964-65	3,228	77	19
1965-66	4,013	101	24
1966-67	2,732	368	124
1967-68	4,509	408	32
April-December 1968	4,474	293	179

Source: Department of Employment and Productivity, Ministry of Labor (May, 1969).

which are carried out by Northern Ireland and the National Coal and National Railway boards, and the number of workers relocated exceeds 5,000 a year. Secondly, vested pension programs inhibit the mobility of many British workers. Accumulated pension credits "lock" many workers into their old jobs. The great majority of pension schemes are not transferable when a worker moves. Finally, housing shortages in areas of economic expansion have constituted a serious barrier to labor mobility in Britain, as in other European countries. There is no disposition on the part of workers in London and other expanding areas to relinquish their claims to housing, for which they may have waited for several years, to newcomers from the development areas. Despite the small number of workers moved, the relocation programs of the Ministry of Labor are well designed to cope with structural unemployment by facilitating the mobility of both unemployed workers and those with skills in urgent demand.

RELOCATION OF WORKERS
IN NORTHERN IRELAND

Northern Ireland has a program for relocating unemployed workers which is similar to but separate from the relocation program administered by the Ministry of Labor in Great Britain. The program is administered by the Ministry of Health and Social Services, which is located in Belfast. Unemployed workers registered at local employment offices, whose prospects of employment in the home area are poor, are eligible for relocation assistance to take up employment in another area in Northern Ireland or in Great Britain proper. Two schemes are provided for relocation of the unemployed-- a temporary transfer scheme which provides certain benefits to unemployed workers with family responsibilities who transfer temporarily to other areas where employment is available, and a permanent resettlement scheme for unemployed workers who are prepared to settle permanently in another area in Northern Ireland or Great Britain.

Overall eligibility criteria are similar to those set under the programs in Great Britain. A worker must be unemployed and have no immediate prospect for employment in the

home area. He must transfer with the approval of a local
office of the Ministry of Health and Social Services and must
transfer beyond daily traveling distance from his present
home. He is ineligible to receive assistance if the new job
pays more than £1,500 a year. (This standard is set to ex-
clude the payment of relocation allowances to technical and
professional workers who could afford the cost of moving and
resettlement.) Allowances are similar to those payable under
the relocation schemes of Great Britain.

An idea of the number of workers moved under the relocation program of Northern Ireland can be gained from
Table 14. The number of returnees also is indicated. Only
those workers who are relocated in and who return from
Great Britain are counted.

It should be emphasized, however, that there is free
movement within the United Kingdom, and these figures
represent only a fraction of the total number of workers
moving within and from Northern Ireland. Nevertheless,
these figures represent unemployed workers, and some idea
of their significance can be obtained by comparing them with
the average monthly number of registered unemployed workers
in Northern Ireland for several of the above years. In 1960,
the average monthly number of unemployed was approximately
35,000; in 1962, the average monthly number was 38,000;
and in 1964, the average monthly number was approximately
39,000. Over the five-year period, approximately 5 percent of the unemployed have been relocated in Great Britain
through the use of relocation allowances.

Approximately 65,000 workers from Northern Ireland
took employment in Great Britain during this five-year period.
This would include 7,309 workers moved under the relocation
programs. The remainder moved without the allowances.
(Workers have to be unemployed to be eligible for relocation
allowances.)

Approximately 15,000 workers returned home after employment in Great Britain and registered as unemployed or
secured employment. This number included 1,804 who received the relocation allowances but returned home after a
period of employment in Great Britain. The return rate of

TABLE 14

Number of Workers Moved Under Relocation Programs
in Northern Ireland, 1960-67

Year	Number Placed in Employment in Great Britain	Number of transferred workers returning from Great Britain
1960	1,655	386
1961	1,905	426
1962	1,051	414
1963	683	200
1964	2,015	378
1965	1,984	294
1966	2,095	407
1967	2,277	395
	13,685	2,900

Source: Employment Division, Ministry of Health and Social Services (1969).

72

25 percent for those receiving relocation allowances can be compared with an overall return rate of about 22 percent.

The movement of unemployed workers from Northern Ireland to Great Britain through the use of relocation allowances might well be much greater but for the effects of a basic deterrent factor. The type of labor is not that which is in short supply in Great Britain. Over 80 percent of the unemployed are unskilled or semi-skilled; but since there is a shortage of unskilled unemployed men only in particular localities in Great Britain, the scope for the movement of unskilled workers from Northern Ireland is limited, and the jobs available to them often are considered to be unattractive, either in pay or in conditions of work.

The Hall report on the economy of Northern Ireland makes the following statements with reference to the use of relocation allowances to ameliorate the problem of unemployment:

The problem of unemployment might be eased by increased migration. To the extent that further migration could be encouraged, it would be possible simultaneously to alleviate the problem of unemployment in Northern Ireland and the shortage of labor in areas such as the Midlands. This may well, moreover, be more economical than encouraging new industries to Northern Ireland. The amount of migration has been less than the natural increase in population and insufficient to reduce local unemployment. [9]

The Hall report also recommends that relocation allowances be increased.

RELOCATION OF WORKERS BY THE NATIONAL COAL BOARD

The third workers relocation program is administered by the National Coal Board. This program pertains to the transfer of unemployed coal miners from areas where coal mines have been shut down or phased out to areas where coal mining is still profitable.

Problems

When the National Coal Board took over control of the coal mining industry in 1947, there were nearly 1,000 pits, employing 750,000 men, in operation. The industry had been suffering for many years from the lack of capital investment, the depression, and high unemployment rates.

From 1947 to 1957, employment in the coal mines stabilized at around 700,000. However, toward the end of 1957 the employment picture began to change for the following reasons:

1.   An increase in the use of other sources of energy, especially oil;

2.   A generally lower level of industrial activity; and

3.   Much greater efficiency in the mining of coal.

Employment in the collieries declined from 705,000 at the end of 1957 to 364,000 at the end of 1968. (Normal attrition and early retirement account for the majority of these workers.) Also by March 1965, 270 collieries employing 212,000 men were losing money. Consequently, the National Coal Board has been concentrating on phasing out the operations of the unprofitable mines and transferring unemployed miners to areas which are still profitable.

The conditions of individual collieries in the same district vary widely but, in general, there are more pits with limited reserves, or which are unprofitable, in Scotland, Northumberland, Durham, Cumberland, and South Wales, while the profitable long-life pits are concentrated mainly in the East and West Midlands and Yorkshire.

The relocation of unemployed coal miners has followed the following pattern: the unemployed miners in Scotland have been employed in mines in Yorkshire, North Staffordshire, and North Wales; unemployed miners in Durham and Northumberland have been employed in mines in North Staffordshire, South Staffordshire, and Yorkshire.

Allowances and Benefits

The allowances and benefits for transferred coal miners are as follows:

For the initial journey to take up employment, all men receive single fare for the initial journey to the new place of employment; an allowance of up to 20 shillings to cover expenses on the initial journey; and payment of wages for working time unavoidably lost while traveling to the new place of employment.

After transfer, the man without dependents receives a settling-in allowance of £5 a week for the first four working weeks and assistance with the cost of lodgings and periodic visits home.

After transfer, the man with dependents who is living away from his old home receives a settling-in allowance of £5 a week for the first four working weeks; a lodging allowance of 70 shillings a week for up to two years; an assistance fare home every month for up to two years (he pays the first 12 shillings, 6 pence of the return fare); and assistance toward the cost of traveling home in case of domestic emergency.

The transferred man whose dependents are with him receives single fares for dependents when they move from the old home to the new and an allowance for dependents aged five or over of up to 20 shillings to cover expenses on the journey (children under five receive one-half this rate); a continuing liability allowance when dependents move to the new district before the removal of household effects and there is a continuing liability in the old district for rent or storage of furniture (this allowance is equal to the actual cost, up to a maximum of 49 shillings per week); the actual cost of household removal; reasonable extra costs of insurance of furniture and effects in transit or storage; a household settlement grant of £50 when the worker and his dependents have established themselves as a settled household in the new area; and a temporary increase in rent allowance when the rent for the house in the new district exceeds the rent for the house in the old by more than 10 shillings a week.

Finally, the National Coal Board makes every effort to get the transfered men and their families housed quickly. This usually means new housing has to be built, since there are waiting lists for rented homes, and only a small minority purchase their own homes. This new construction is primarily the responsibility of the local authorities, who receive a government subsidy of £ 24 a year for 60 years for every house built for a man moving to meet the needs of industry, and a further National Coal Board subsidy of up to £ 30 a year for 15 years, provided the houses are for miners. If the local authorities are unable or unwilling to build, then the Coal Board, through its subsidiary Coal Industry Housing Association, constructs the houses and lets them at rents equivalent to those of the local housing authorities.

The National Coal Board redesigned and expanded an interdivisional transfer scheme in 1962, offering remployment to coal miners from Scotland, Northumberland, Cumberland, and Durham, mainly in Yorkshire and the Midlands, where their services could be utilized. In 1964 a supplementary scheme for long-distance re-entrants was introduced, covering unemployed coal miners and re-entrants to the industry from other employment.

Although the program is relatively new, approximately 10, 000 coal miners have been moved since 1962, and the average expenditure per year has been £ 300, 000 ($720, 000). [10] Twenty percent of all workers transferred under the Coal Board's relocation scheme leave their new jobs to return home or to take another job in the new area. The major reasons for workers' leaving their new jobs were lack of housing and homesickness.

THE BRITISH RAILWAYS SYSTEM

The British Railways System has a program for relocating unemployed railway workers which is similar in every respect to that of the National Coal Board. Employment in the railroad industry of Great Britain has decreased from 648, 740 in 1948 to 340, 000 in 1967. [11] Recent decisions

foresee a shrinkage to about 250,000 by 1975. This shrinkage will occur in the central industrial areas as well as the
periphery, freeing some 60,000 productive workers along with
the older immobile ones.

Approximately 1,500 workers were moved per year during
the period 1962-65. In addition to the closure of railway
workshops, a number of stations were closed. However,
many major improvements in efficiency were made, and the
number of workers relocated averaged less than 1,000 a
year from 1965 to 1967. In the future, some railway sectors
are expected to absorb more workers, not fewer.

SUMMARY

The British postwar record on full employment in relation to earlier experiences in this century has been quite
good. Considerable weight has been attached to a low unemployment rate in the formulation of British economic
policies. However, successive governments have failed in
their attempts to render compatible the irreconcilable objectives of maintaining full employment and of preventing inflation, or at least their effects on the balance of payments.
The low level of unemployment has contributed, via rising
prices and money incomes, to the deterioration in the balance
of payments and an impairment in the efficiency of the economy
--and thus in the rate of economic growth. It would appear
that an increase in unemployment is necessary to check inflation and to prevent the emergence of another balance of
payments crisis. Then attention could be concentrated on a
more efficient allocation of labor.

Although the national unemployment rate has been kept
below 3 percent for virtually all of the postwar period, regional
unemployment continues to exist at rates which are considerably above the national average. This existence of high
regional unemployment rates tends to repudiate, to a certain
extent, the argument advanced by many economists that unemployment is attributable to a deficiency in aggregate demand and can be reduced substantially by fiscal and monetary
policies that increase demand. Although it is true that

expansionary economic policies have kept the national unemployment rate low in Great Britain, the unevenness in
unemployment between regions indicates that a certain amount
of unemployment can be attributable to structural changes
and the mismatching of workers and jobs. Expansionary
policies have also been accompanied by inflation. It can be
argued that policies which have as their objective increasing
aggregate demand in order to lower the unemployment rate
to some irreducible minimum cause inflation and a dis-
equilibrium in the labor market.

It is significant to note that unemployment rates in the
less prosperous areas of Great Britain and Northern Ireland
have shown little improvement over the period from 1952 to
1969 despite expansionary national economic policies and the
use of a wide range of employment-creating grants which are
available to business firms.

There is strong academic support in Great Britain for
moving unemployed workers to areas where employment is
available. [12] However, the British government regards the
relocation of unemployed workers as only a partial solution
to the problem of regional unemployment. The total number
of workers moved under the relocation schemes of the Ministry of Labor and the nationalized coal and railway industries
is less than 10, 000 a year, and the total estimated cost of relocating these workers is around £ 1. 2 million a year. Although the number of relocated workers is very small relative to the size of the British labor force, several factors
exist which inhibit the effectiveness of relocation:

1.   Lack of available housing is the major deterrent
to the success of the various relocation programs.

2.   Geographic distances are a minor deterrent to
the mobility of labor. Movements from one area to another
entail distances which are less than movements within many
American states.

3.   Concentrations of population into the more prosperous areas of Great Britain constitutes a major national
problem. British regional employment policies attempt to
bring jobs to areas of unemployment in order to maintain a
population balance between regions.

NOTES

1. See "Report of the President's Committee on Measuring Employment and Unemployment, 1962," Appendix A.

2. Sir William Beveridge, Full Employment in a Free Society (London: George Allen & Unwin, Ltd., 1944), p. 29.

3. British White Paper No. 2188, An Inquiry into the Scottish Economy, (London: Her Majesty's Stationery Office), p. 47.

4. Employment and Productivity Gazette (London: Department of Employment and Productivity, May, 1969), 456-457.

5. See British White Paper No. 3310, The Development Areas: Regional Employment Premiums (London: Her Majesty's Stationery Office, 1967), p. 6.

6. Pt. I, sec. 5, pp. 4, 5.

7. See Local Employment Act of 1960, pt. I, sec. 6, pp. 4, 5.

8. See Martin Schnitzer, "Programs for Relocating Workers Used by Governments of Selected Countries," Joint Economic Committee Monograph, Congress of the United States (Washington, D.C.: Government Printing Office, 1965), p. 13.

9. British White Paper No. 1835, Report of the Joint Working Party on the Economy of Northern Ireland (London: Her Majesty's Stationery Office, 1962), p. 12, par. 33; see also p. 52, par. 177; p. 54, pars. 184-187.

10. Information provided by the National Coal Board.

11. The Economist (Dec. 23, 1967).

12.   The following publications may be cited as examples: H. Makower, J. Marshak, and H. W. Robinson, Studies in the Mobility of Labor, Analysis for Great Britain, Pt. II, Oxford Economic Papers (Sept. 1960); A. T. Peacock and D. G. M. Dosser, "The New Attack on Localized Unemployment," Lloyds Bank Review (Jan. 1960); and H. W. Richardson and E. G. West, "Must We Always Take Work to the Workers," Lloyds Bank Review (Jan. 1964).   Also see British White Paper No. 1835, Report of the Joint Working Party on the Economy of Northern Ireland (London: Her Majesty's Stationery Office, 1962), pp. 52-54.

CHAPTER **4** CANADA

INTRODUCTION

In few countries of the world is the problem of geographic distance more acute than in Canada. It has a land area larger than the United States and a population about the size of that of California. Many areas of population are 500 to 1,000 miles from any city of any size. The cost of moving in Great Britain, or even in Sweden, would involve a distance of probably no more than a maximum of 400 miles, with the average distance probably less than half of that. Even in the United States, much movement is made between areas within-state or to areas in nearby states. However, in Canada, with a small population and a large land area, almost any move will involve considerable distance and cost.

Except for the language dichotomy between English and French, there is a strong similarity between the United States and Canada. Both have a federal form of government. In Canada, the provinces have a considerable degree of autonomy. In fact, many of the social welfare programs, which are normally regarded as the function of the national government, are undertaken by provincial governments in Canada. The standard of living is very high in Canada. In 1965, based on taxable and non-taxable returns, average Canadian per capita income was $4,200 per return. Average family income was $6,400 and median family income was $5,820.[1] However, there is a distinct variation in terms of income among the ten Canadian provinces, with Ontario, Quebec, and British Columbia having the highest per capita and per family incomes, and Newfoundland, Prince Edward Island, and New Brunswick having the lowest incomes.

UNEMPLOYMENT

Although the Canadian unemployment rate has been low
in recent years, the problem of regional unemployment exists.
In 1964 the average unemployment rate for Canada was 4.7
percent. (The Canadian measure of unemployment includes
all those who are looking for work in a survey week and who
do not find work. Also included are persons temporarily
away from their jobs during the whole of the survey week and
who are looking for work. In addition to the active seekers,
there are included persons who would look for work except
that they are: (1) temporarily ill; (2) on prolonged layoff;
and (3) under the impression that no work is available in the
community or in their particular skill. Persons on temporary
layoff--subject to recall within 30 days--also are classified
as unemployed.) Broken down by regions, however, the unemployment rate was as follows: Atlantic (includes Maritime
Provinces), 7.8 percent; Quebec, 6.3 percent; Ontario, 3.3
percent; Prairie, 3 percent; and Pacific, 5.3 percent. In
1968 the average unemployment rate for Canada was 4.8 percent; and by regions the unemployment rate was Atlantic,
7.5 percent; Quebec, 6.5 percent; Ontario, 3.5 percent;
Prairie, 2.9 percent; and Pacific, 5.9 percent.

In Canada, there is a very high rate of seasonal unemployment. At its peak in the months of January, February,
and March, seasonal unemployment averages some 300,000
workers higher than in the summer months. In 1968, the
seasonal rate of unemployment for Canada ranged from a high
of 6.4 percent in February to 3.3 percent in September. For
Prince Edward Island, the seasonal rate of unemployment
ranged from a high of 17.1 percent in January to a low of 2.5
percent in August. In New Brunswick, the rates varied from
11.7 percent to 4.1 percent. Moreover, there has also been
a secular decline in employment in three industries that have
very large seasonal fluctuations in employment: agriculture,
forestry, and fishing. Over the period from 1948 to 1967,
employment in agriculture declined from 1,095,000 to 545,000
and employment in fishing and forestry declined from 105,000
to 77,000.

The problem of regional unemployment is limited primarily to the Atlantic region and portions of Quebec. The

economy of the Atlantic region has been geared to a resource base which either has eroded away or has suffered
from a lack of adequate demand. Unemployment in such
primary industries as mining, forestry, fishing, and trapping
--all of which are indigenous to the Atlantic region--has
averaged 15 percent of total employment in these industries.
In Newfoundland, which is a province with considerable unemployment in fishing, the unemployment rate for 1968 was
in excess of 10 percent, compared with the average unemployment rate of 4. 8 percent for Canada. [2] For the first
five months of 1969, the unemployment rate in Newfoundland
averaged around 13 percent.

The average unemployment rate for Canada and for the
10 Canadian provinces afford an important comparison, which
is presented in Table 15.

There is considerable variation in unemployment between regions within provinces. For example, Manitoba
had an average unemployment rate of 3. 4 percent for 1968,
but three areas within the province--Brandon, Dauphin, and
Selkirk--had an average unemployment rate in excess of
9 percent. Saskatchewan had the lowest unemployment rate
in Canada, but four regions - Lloydminster, North Battle-
ford, Prince Albert, and Yorkton--had unemployment rates
in excess of 8 percent. In Prince Edward Island, seasonal
unemployment rates for Charlottetown and Summerside exceed 20 percent for the winter months. In addition to this
high rate of unemployment, there is a substantial degree of
underemployment in Prince Edward Island, Nova Scotia,
Newfoundland, and New Brunswick. In Prince Edward Island,
output per worker in all sectors is well below the national
average, and by as much as 50 percent in agriculture.

In 1963, the Area Redevelopment Agency was set up
within the newly established Department of Industry to work
with other federal, provincial, and municipal agencies and
with business interests in problem areas. Thirty-five out
of 200 local labor areas were designated as development
areas. Benefits given to manufacturing and processing enterprises locating in the designated development areas included
important tax concessions: exemption of new enterprises
from the Canadian corporate income tax for a period of three
years following the start of commercial operations and an

TABLE 15

Average Unemployment Rates in Canadian Provinces, 1968

Province	Unemployment Rate
Newfoundland	10.3%
Nova Scotia	5.8
Prince Edward Island	7.1
New Brunswick	7.3
Quebec	6.5
Ontario	3.5
Manitoba	3.4
Saskatchewan	2.4
Alberta	2.9
British Columbia	6.0
Canada	4.8

Source: Dominion Bureau of Statistics (Aug., 1969).

accelerated tax write-off on investments in buildings, machinery, and equipment.

In 1967, new criteria were established for development areas. To be eligible for such a classification, an area has to have an unemployment rate at least twice the national average for the last five years, or an unemployment rate of at least one and one-half times the national average and a growth rate in employment of less than two- thirds of the national average. Another criterion which may be applied to an area is an average annual non-farm family income of less than $4, 250, or an average annual income of $3, 000 or less for 40 percent or more of the area's non-farm families.

POVERTY

On the basis of budget data devised by the Dominion Bureau of Statistics, an attempt has been made to quantify the number of low-income families in Canada. The basic criterion used to determine low incomes was an expenditure on food, clothing, and shelter which totaled 70 percent of family income. A sample taken in 1959 of families living in population centers of 15, 000 or more revealed that on the average, families of various sizes tended to spend 50 percent of their income on food, clothing, and shelter. Families that spent 70 percent on the basic necessities had little left to spend on other needs. In other words, their discretionary income was small, and they enjoyed little better than a subsistence level of living.

This survey resulted in the selection of the following figures as the cut-off points for the designation "low-income": $1, 500 for a single person; $2, 500 for a family of two; $3, 000 for a family of three; $3, 500 for a family of four; and $4, 000 for a family of five or more. (These incomes are relatively higher than incomes suggested for the United States because Canadian incomes average about 85 percent of U. S. incomes.) Individuals and families with incomes below these levels were assumed to follow the 70 percent expenditure pattern. The above income criteria were applied to both urban and rural non-farm families.

In 1961, 25.3 percent of all Canadian non-farm families and 43.5 pércent of all individuals had incomes that fell below the above standards. The families contained 4,163,000 persons, approximately 27 percent of the population. This however denotes low income, but not necessarily poverty.

The number of low-income non-farm family units in 1961 varied considerably by province, as Table 16 indicates.

If the same low-income criteria are applied to 1965 income data for non-farm families and individuals, the following breakdown would be obtained:[3]

      1.   37 percent of all individuals made less than $1,500;

      2.   23.7 percent of families with two persons made less than $2,500;

      3.   14.8 percent of all families with three persons made less than $3,000;

      4.   11.8 percent of families with four persons made less than $3,500; and

      5.   15.4 percent of families with five or more persons made less than $4,000.

By applying the following criteria to 1961 census data, Nariman K. Dhalla has classified Canadian families on the basis of poor versus non-poor.[4]

      1.   An annual income of $3,000 for non-farm families.

      2.   An annual income of $1,500 for non-farm individuals not in families.

      3.   An annual gross farm income of $2,500.

      4.   An annual income of $1,200 for farm workers.

TABLE 16

Percentage of Low-Income Families, by Province, 1961

Newfoundland	55.7
Prince Edward Island	49.2
Nova Scotia	40.3
New Brunswick	43.5
Quebec	27.9
Ontario	18.6
Manitoba	26.1
Saskatchewan	34.8
Alberta	22.9
British Columbia	21.3
Canada	25.3

Source: J. R. Podoluk, unpublished paper, Central Research and Development Staff, Dominion Bureau of Statistics (1965).

On the basis of these criteria, in 1961, 847,940 families
with 2,915,672 persons; 687,857 persons not in families; and
221,866 farm households with 1,020,584 persons--a total of
4,624,113 persons, or 25.4 percent of the Canadian popu-
lation--were classified as poor. [5]   The percentage of families
making less than $3,000 a year ranged from 51.2 percent in
Newfoundland to 17.8 percent in Ontario, and the percentage
of individuals not in families making less than $1,500 a year
ranged from 73.8 percent in Newfoundland to 44.9 percent in
Ontario.   Based on urban-rural residence, the percentage
of families making less than $3,000 a year ranged from 18.9
percent for metropolitan areas to 42.5 percent for rural non-
farm areas. [6]

The characteristics of families with incomes of less than
$3,000 and individuals with incomes of less than $1,500 are
easy to identify:

1.   Sex.   53.7 percent of all families with income
of less than $3,000 were headed by females; and females
accounted for 57.2 percent of all individuals making less
than $1,500.

2.   Education, or lack of it.   Two-thirds of the
847,940 families had an elementary school education or less.

3.   Occupation.   In 1961, 34.9 percent of families
headed by an unskilled laborer made less than $3,000 a year,
compared with 13.7 percent for skilled and semi-skilled
workers.   Low incomes are also prevalent among farmers.
In 1961, 46.1 percent of commercial and non-commercial
farms had gross incomes of $2,500 or less.   The percentage
ranged from 84 percent in Newfoundland to 32.3 percent in
Saskatchewan.

4.   Age.   In 1961, 53 percent of family heads 65
or over and 32.3 percent of family heads under 25 made less
than $3,000 a year.

5.   Race.   In 1961, 17,230 out of 26,977 Indian
families made less than $2,500 a year.

6.   Region.   In 1961, 51.2 percent of families and
73.8 percent of individuals made less than $3,000 and $1,500,

respectively, in Newfoundland; 44. 8 percent and 67. 1 percent in Prince Edward Island; to 17. 8 percent and 44. 9 percent in Ontario; and 20. 7 percent and 43. 9 percent in Alberta.

In 1961, the Agricultural Rehabilitation and Development
Act (ARDA) was passed. The purpose of the act was to develop a set of programs which were directed toward the al-
leviation of low incomes in rural areas. These programs
are federal-provincial in nature. The provinces have the
responsibility of initiating programs, implementing them,
and paying half of the cost. Projects include the promotion
of more productive use of marginal and sub-marginal land
for agricultural production and the preparation of comprehensive plans, with the participation of local residents through
rural development committees. There are soil and water
conservation projects that place emphasis on developments
that encompass resource management throughout an entire
watershed or river valley.

In 1966 the Fund for Rural Economic Development (FRED)
was established by an act of Parliament. It permits a federal
expenditure of $300 million from consolidated revenues over
a five-year period, and is designed to promote rural development. In the same year the Canadian government and
the province of New Brunswick signed an agreement under
the provisions of FRED to develop the northeast region of
New Brunswick. The provincial government had to match
expenditures with the national government. Basic measures
to be accomplished under the agreement include the expansion
and modernization of school facilities, the provision of vocational training schools which will provide training for 700
workers a year, grants of up to $2, 400 to encourage the move-
ment of families out of isolated areas to more viable economic
areas, the construction of several thousand housing units in
major population centers in the northeast area to encourage
movement from nonviable rural areas, and the expansion and
development of the off-shore fishing industry. A number of
small public investment projects will also be undertaken to
provide local employment opportunities for seasonally employed workers.

In 1967, the Canadian government and the province of
Manitoba signed an agreement to develop the Interlake area
of Manitoba. Funds on a matching basis are provided to

support programs initiated under the Interlake Comprehensive Rural Development Plan.   Support is provided for
vocational training and mobility assistance.   Emphasis also
is placed on the development of water conservation and control projects, and the purchase of marginal lands from low-
income farmers.   Special development areas are also being
developed for the purpose of creating growth centers.

RELOCATION ASSISTANCE

The Canadian government had three separate programs
of relocation assistance.

1.   The government (National Employment Service)
provided transportation assistance, including meals and
lodging, on a non-recoverable basis, to unemployed workers
in designated labor surplus areas who moved to employment
in other areas.   The workers' dependents and household
effects, including a mobile home, also were moved at public
expense.   To be eligible, a worker had to pass a means test--
he had to demonstrate an inability to pay such costs himself.

2.   An employer wishing to recruit workers beyond
commuting distance from his operation could authorize the
National Employment Service to advance, on a refundable
basis, travel expenses to selected workers to enable them
to proceed to employment.   This was done in connection with
the regular clearance of labor through local offices of the
National Employment Service.   The employer had to reim-
burse the National Employment Service.

3.   The third program under which workers were
moved with all or part of their transportation paid was the
Dominion-Provincial Farm Labor Movement.   Under this
program, the workers paid part of the cost and the federal
and provincial governments shared the balance.   This program applied to workers recruited in one area of Canada to
assist with farm crops in another area.   In recent years,
workers have been recruited in the Maritime Provinces for
employment in Ontario as farmhands, vegetable and fruit
pickers, and cannery and fruit-processing workers.

The Manpower Mobility Program was introduced by Prime Minister Pearson in May, 1965. It superseded the movement at public expense of workers from designated areas; but the advancing of transportation costs on behalf of employers who authorized them was continued, as was the seasonal movement of workers. Under the new program, the means test was dropped, and loans were made available at interest rates which were not to exceed 6 percent to workers for whom employment could not be found in the home area but could be found in another area. Grants also were made available for the long-term unemployed.

Loans covered the cost of transportation of the worker and/or his dependents, the cost of transporting his household effects (including the cost of moving a mobile home), and a resettlement allowance which was not to exceed $1,000. Grants included the same benefits that were applicable to the worker who qualified for a loan; however, if the worker was without dependents, he was eligible for a grant for his transportation only.

The Manpower Mobility Program was revised in April, 1967, to expand its scope and liberalize its terms. The response to the original program had been disappointing. During the entire period that the program had been in effect (December, 1965, to April, 1967), fewer than 1,500 workers moved with grants and 1,300 with loans. In part, this reflected a lag in public knowledge about the terms of the program. Also, eligibility requirements were fairly stringent. For example, benefits were available only to workers who were unemployed for four or more months out of six. Moreover, the program discriminated against men who had taken odd jobs in order to support their family. The obligation to repay loans discouraged many potential relocatees.

New provisions eliminated loans and the four-out-of-six-months unemployment prerequisite for relocation grants. Eligibility requirements were changed to include the following groups of workers:[7]

1. Unemployed workers who find prospects for full-time employment to be unpromising in the home area. Any person who is unemployed, or has been notified of his permanent lay-off, is eligible for relocation allowances.

2.   Underemployed workers who have worked less than 30 hours a week for 13 weeks before the week in which application is made for relocation grants.

The Manpower Mobility Program covers all of Canada. It is available to unemployed workers wishing to move to employment beyond commuting distance from their homes and to certain other groups of workers, including underemployed workers, particularly from rural areas.   Relocation allowances payable to underemployed workers would cover a considerable part of the Canadian labor force employed in agriculture, fishing, forestry, and other seasonal or primary activities.   The Department of Manpower and Immigration is responsible for the administration of relocation grants. This responsibility covers not only payment of the grant but also actual supervision of the relocation.   The latter involves manpower officers in both the supply and the receiving areas.

The following benefits are payable under the current Manpower Mobility Program:

1.   Exploratory or travel grants, which are designed to encourage unemployed workers to search for jobs in the nearest area having better prospects of employment. These grants cover a worker's travel expenses and provide his dependents with a living allowance for up to four weeks while he searches.   (The allowance varies by province and region from a minimum of $12 a week for one dependent to a maximum of $40 a week for three or more dependents.)   The travel allowance is based on the cost of transportation by the cheapest public carrier (bus, train) from the home area to the area where the job is available.   Also included is an allowance for meals and overnight accommodations, if necessary.   Underemployed workers also are entitled to receive exploratory grants.   There is no obligation on the part of a worker to take employment.

2.   Trainee travel grants are paid to workers enrolled under the Adult Occupational Training Act.   These grants cover travel expenses to and from training centers in communities which are removed from a trainee's home. The cost of meals and lodging are included in the grant.

3.   Relocation grants are payable to workers who move. They include an amount which is equal to the cost of transportation for a worker and his dependents by the most economical means from the locality in which they live to the place where employment has been obtained. The grant includes allowances for meals and overnight accommodations for a worker and his dependents while in transit.

An amount equal to the actual cost of moving the household and personal effects of a worker and his dependents is included in the relocation grant. In addition, there is a re-settlement grant which is not to exceed $200 for the worker, $200 for his spouse, and $100 for each dependent other than the spouse--the total settlement allowance not to exceed $1,000. A worker without dependents is eligible for a settlement allowance of $200.

As a further incentive to mobility, housing grants of $500 are given to workers who sell their old homes and purchase new homes in the relocation area. The purpose of the housing grant is to compensate a worker at least partially for any loss incurred in selling his home in the home area.

The results of the Manpower Mobility Program have been impressive, considering the fact that it has been in effect for only a short period of time. During the fiscal year 1967-68, close to 6,000 unemployed workers received relocation grants, compared with 2,800 workers who received grants or loans under the previous relocation program, which was in effect for 16 months. [8] The 6,000 relocatees represented about 4 percent of the total number of unemployed workers in Canada. In addition, 4,700 workers received exploratory grants to search for new employment, and of these 30 percent took relocation grants to move their families. Financial expenditures on the mobility program amounted to more than $3 million for the fiscal year 1967-68, over double the expenditures made under the grant-loan program of the preceding 16 months. In addition, some 18,000 workers received trainee travel grants.

Table 17 presents the total cost of the Canadian Manpower Mobility Program and the number of workers relocated since the program was started in December, 1965. It is

TABLE 17

Expenditures and Relocations Under the Canadian
Manpower Mobility Program

Fiscal Year	Workers Involved	Total Expenditures
1966-67		
Loans	1,267	$358,309
Grants	1,481	930,132
1967-68		
Relocation	6,200	2,588,856
Exploratory	4,676	118,672
Trainee travel	18,227	351,566
1968-69		
Relocation	6,591	3,329,048
Exploratory	6,351	211,218
Trainee travel	31,727	561,520

Source: Planning and Evaluation Branch, Department of Manpower and Immigration.

necessary to remember that there are two stages to the pro-
gram--the grant-loan stage, which lasted for 16 months, and
the current stage, involving grants only, which began in 1967.

In March, 1968, the Department of Manpower and Immigration made effective a further amendment in the mobility
regulations extending grants to underemployed workers, i. e.,
those employed for less than 30 hours a week, or in jobs
where their main skills are not being used. This amendment
did not have an effect on the total relocations for 1968-69 because its implementation was subjected to some delay. However, the impact on total relocation could be considerable,
particularly in the agricultural sector of the Canadian economy.

The distribution of relocation grants follows no particular
regional pattern. Table 18 presents the number of relocation
grant recipients by region of origin. In general, the region
of relocation was the same as the region of origin, with the
exception of the Atlantic region, where the majority of the
relocatees were transferred to Ontario and other regions.

In general, the flow of relocatees follows normal Canadian
mobility patterns: from the farms, fishing villages, and rural
areas into the towns and cities. The majority of relocatees
are under 34 years of age. Not surprisingly, given the high
incidence of unemployment among younger workers, the largest
single group is under 25 years of age. Almost one-quarter of
all relocation grants go to workers with four or more dependents. Most moves involve distances of less than 500 miles,
and over three-quarters of the workers find jobs in their own
provinces. Relocation grants average $600 per relocatee,
and exploratory grants $60. [9]

Canada's relocation program can be compared with the
established programs of the western European countries. In
general, the incentives to move are more generous than those
of most European programs. In terms of the number of
workers moved with relocation grants, the 6, 200 workers relocated in 1967-68 would be less than the total for Sweden and
the United Kingdom, but more than the total for France and
West Germany. However, the Swedish and British relocation
programs have been in effect for a much longer period of
time.

TABLE 18

Manpower Mobility Program Relocation Grant Recipients,
by Region of Origin

Region	Fiscal Year 1967-68	Fiscal Year 1968-69
Atlantic	959	705
Quebec	1,472	2,242
Ontario	2,788	2,732
Prairie	508	490
Pacific	473	422
Canada	6,200	6,591

Source: Planning and Evaluation Branch, Department of Manpower and Immigration.

Although the Manpower Mobility Program has been in operation for only a short period of time, some results are available for analysis. The basic factor in evaluating any relocation program is not the amount of money spent or the total number of workers moved, but how effective relocation is in enhancing the productive capabilities of the workers who move. Preliminary studies made by the Planning and Evaluation Branch of the Department of Manpower and Immigration indicate that only two out of three relocation moves could be considered successful in terms of the worker's remaining in the demand area. Less than two-fifths of the workers receiving exploratory grants secure steady employment. However, several factors are responsible for the rather high return rate. In some cases, workers have been placed in mining and related primary occupations which have high turnover rates among all types of workers. Relocatees with sporadic work records also are likely to return to the home area. Homesickness, the lack of adequate housing facilities, and certain sociological factors also present a barrier to successful relocation on the part of many workers.[10]

However, the Manpower Mobility Program is producing some desirable results. The incidence and length of unemployment are reduced for workers who otherwise would be locked into stagnating or declining industries or occupations. Proportionately more families are being moved from depressed areas than would otherwise occur. The productive output of the workers moved increased by 10 to 15 percent. There is a faster and more efficient filling of existing job vacancies, which helps to reduce the real cost of output. The mobility program is regarded as an integral part of a broad manpower program which involves job training, the relocation of industry, and the elimination of sub-marginal farms. It should be stressed that these benefits cannot be measured exclusively in terms of the present generation. Relocation, by bringing families out of depressed or rural areas, is expected to broaden the aspirations and opportunities for the young.[11]

A major cost-benefit analysis of the Manpower Mobility Program was started in 1969. Its purpose is to estimate the net benefits from moving workers during the 1967-68 fiscal year. Personal information on each relocatee is matched against a set of a priori expectations involving the move to yield an estimate of expected net benefits per relocatee. Preliminary reports suggest a very favorable net benefit ratio for the program.

The question of regional dislocation has yet to arise because the Manpower Mobility Program is relatively new and the number of workers moved is small. Large-scale exodus from an area can raise the marginal productivity of the workers left behind, or it can discourage new investment and cause existing social capital to fall into disrepair. Problems of inadequate housing and social services may be caused by the migration of workers to areas where labor is in short supply. However, the Canadian program is relocating unemployed or under employed workers who contribute little to the growth of a region, and is putting them into areas where their contribution to output is undeniably higher. Most of these workers and their families constituted more of a burden on the social capital of a depressed area than a source of revenue.

Financial inducements to encourage the location of industry in areas with above-average unemployment are more likely to be successful in a country the size of Great Britain than in Canada. In Great Britain, for example, no problem area is far removed from transportation facilities and market areas. In Canada, the reverse is true. What this means in terms of Canadian manpower policies is that diversification is necessary. Although attempts are being made to create employment and industrial opportunities in areas that offer some chance for viable economic growth, relocation assistance is being used as an integral part of total manpower policies.

SUMMARY

Canada has a large land area and a small population. Although the standard of living is high and the unemployment rate has declined from previous years, there are significant rural-urban disparities in income, and above-average unemployment rates continue to exist in many areas. Rural-urban income disparities are compounded by geographic variations. Many farm families are subject to the double disadvantage of living in one of the lower-income provinces and depending for their livelihood on a declining industry. Seasonal unemployment is high and contributes to the low incomes of many families. Also, unemployment rates vary considerably between and within provinces.

Prior to 1965, the Canadian government had a relocation program for unemployed workers which was based on a means test. The number of workers moved at public expense was small. In the fiscal year 1964-65, the total cost of the relocation program was $43,127. However, this situation was changed with the introduction of the Manpower Mobility Program in 1965. The means test was eliminated and the relocation program was placed on a grant-loan basis. A graduated resettlement allowance of up to $1,000 was made available. As a major part of the government's total manpower program, the Manpower Mobility Program was designed to maintain full employment and ensure a better utilization of manpower resources. The program was extended to unemployed workers in all areas of Canada.

In 1967, the Manpower Mobility Program was amended. Several restrictive provisions, including the loan arrangement, were dropped and the grant provisions were made more attractive. Exploratory grants were introduced to enable unemployed workers to look for work in areas where employment opportunities were available. To help offset losses incurred in selling a house in the home area, relocatees were provided a cash grant of $500. In 1968, the program was extended to cover underemployed workers.

There has been a considerable increase in the cost and in the number of workers moved in the Canadian relocation program since 1965. As mentioned above, the cost for the fiscal year 1964-65 was $43,127. Fewer than 500 workers were moved. During the fiscal year 1968-69, more than 6,000 workers were moved at a cost of $3,329,048. The number relocated is small relative to the total number of persons moving between regions each year. Nevertheless, preliminary investigations indicate favorable results, and the extension of relocation grants to underemployed workers should increase the cost of the program and number of workers moved.

NOTES

1.   Dominion Bureau of Statistics, Bulletin 13-528, Distribution of Income in Canada by Size (1965), p. 15.

2.   Data provided by the Dominion Bureau of Statistics.

3.   Dominion Bureau of Statistics, Bulletin 13-528, Distribution of Income in Canada by Size (1965).

4.   Nariman K. Dhalla, These Canadians (Montreal: McGraw-Hill Co. of Canada ·Ltd., 1966), pp. 201-203.

5.   Ibid., p. 208.

6.   Ibid., pp. 209-213.

7.   See The Canada Gazette, Pt. II, Vol. 101; Appropriation Acts, "Manpower Mobility Regulations," April 26, 1967, Pt. II, Vol. 102; Appropriation Acts, "Manpower Mobility Regulations, Amended," February 8, 1968, Pt. II, Vol. 102; Appropriation Acts, "Manpower Mobility Regulations of 1967, Amended," June 19, 1968.

8.   Data provided by the Planning and Evaluation Branch, Department of Manpower and Immigration.

9.   Data provided by the Planning and Evaluation Branch.

10.   "The Manpower Mobility Program," a paper delivered at the Round Table on Manpower Mobility by W. R. Dymond, Assistant Deputy Minister, Department of Manpower and Immigration (Sept., 1968).

11.   Ibid., p. 13.

CHAPTER 5 RELOCATION PROGRAMS IN OTHER COUNTRIES

INTRODUCTION

Relocation assistance programs exist in all of the western European countries. In general, they cover the cost of transportation from the home area to the new place of employment, the cost of the removal of furniture and household effects, and a starting or settling-in allowance. A family allowance also is given by most of the countries. Some countries allow an unemployed worker assistance for transportation to look over the location and interview for a job, as well as furnishing the final cost of movement to the job.

The western European countries possess certain common characteristics:

1. The land area is usually so small that movement to a new job entails no significant transportation costs. For example, the area of Belgium is 11,779 square miles, the area of Holland is 12,616 square miles, and the area of Denmark is 16,600 square miles. The combined land areas of the three countries is smaller than the state of Virginia or the state of Illinois. The maximum length of Holland from north to south is 190 miles; its maximum width is 160 miles.

2. The unemployment problems in these countries are similar to those in Sweden, Great Britain, and Canada. Although national unemployment rates usually have been kept at low levels through the use of government fiscal, monetary, and manpower policies, all of the countries have certain areas in which unemployment is well above the national average. There is much similarity, for example, between Norway and Sweden, in that much of the unemployment and lack of economic growth is concentrated in the northern part of the country and considerable distances separate this part from

the population centers and growth areas. Seasonal unemployment is a very important problem in both countries. Unemployment during the winter months is at a rate which is twice the national average.

3.   Although relocation assistance programs in the western European countries have been in existence since the end of the Second World War, the number of workers moved relative to the total number of unemployed workers is small, with the possible exception of Norway. This can be explained by the high level of employment which has existed in western Europe for the last 20 years, and by the lack of geographic distance involved in a typical employment move.

FRANCE

Although the rate of unemployment in France has been low--averaging less than 3 percent during most of the post-war period--there are several problems:

1.   Rapid modernization of French agriculture has been accompanied by a movement of workers from the farms to industry and commerce. Although this movement has been widespread, there is still a surplus of farmers and farm workers. Moreover, there are considerable regional variations in income, with such departments as Ardèche and Savoie having an average farm income which is less than one-half the average farm income for the most prosperous departments: Moselle, Oise, and Maine et Loire. [1] The French government is trying to encourage the exodus of small farmers from unprofitable farming areas, particularly Brittany, which suffers from overpopulation. (The French are moving farm workers from the less prosperous farms in Brittany and southern France to the larger farms around the areas of Paris and Lyons. Small marginal farms are being combined into large farms.)

2.   Employment in several industries has been affected adversely by technological change. One is the ship-building industry (Nantes, Saint-Nazaire, La Seyne, and

Port de Bouc). Another is the iron mines (Pyrénées-
Orientales, Ariège). There has been a decline in employment in the textile industry in such areas as the Vosges.
Employment in certain coal mining areas (Decazeville) also
has declined. Other areas in France with a large number
of small firms--construction, clothing, and textiles--have
been affected by plant closures.

The unemployment rate, which was stable at around 2
percent from 1960 to 1966, increased sharply in 1967, to 2.8
percent by December. In 1968, the unemployment rate went
above 3 percent and remained there for most of the year. [2]
This increase affected certain areas and industries more than
others. Textile production continued to decline, adding to
unemployment in the textile industry. Automobile production
decreased by 13 percent during 1967.

3.   The establishment of the Common Market has
caused some problems. Although the rapid reduction in
tariff barriers between the member nations has been a
powerful factor in the modernization and expansion of each
national economy, major structural changes have been
brought about by this expansion. These changes have been
seen in France in such industries as farm machinery and
coal mining.

Relocation Assistance

The use of relocation assistance in France started with
the decrees of September 14 and December 6, 1954, which
created the Economic and Social Development Fund. Under
this fund, allowances are made available to workers affected
by plant closures, reconversions, or mergers. They include the reimbursement of travel and removal expenses
and a resettlement allowance. French employment offices
have to make every effort to find employment locally for
displaced workers, but can grant relocation allowances if
local employment is unavailable. The employment offices in
both the home and the demand area have to agree to the transfer.

National Employment Fund

Under the National Employment Fund of 1964, provision for relocation allowances has been extended to unemployed workers registered with the national employment service who are obliged to move from an area where unemployment exists to an area where employment is available. (The entire Paris area is excluded as a receiving area because although there is a shortage of labor there, problems of congestion and inadequate housing make the social problems involved in absorbing more workers outweigh the benefits derived by moving workers into Paris.) The framework of the National Employment Fund is defined by the law of December 18, 1963. [3] The law has been supplemented by several decrees (which are mentioned later). The basic purpose of the fund is to provide protection to workers who are affected adversely by structural changes in the French economy. The fund has several forms of assistance available to workers who are unemployed or who will lose their jobs within a given time period:

1.   Assistance is provided for job retraining. Workers are provided with a minimum income as close as possible to their former salary. Allowances are calculated on an hourly rate; they are designed to guarantee workers in the training program 80 percent of their previous average wage.

2.   Assistance is provided to help workers leave regions with an established or foreseen labor surplus and settle in areas with a labor shortage. It includes transfer allowances based on the distance of the move involved; expenses for housing in the new area (the combination of these two allowances is from two to six months' wages at the guaranteed minimum wage rate); reimbursement of travel expenses for workers and members of their families; and reimbursement of moving expenses.

These two forms of assistance have three common features: They are paid by the French government; they are made without regard to geographical or occupational consideration; and they are made on an individual basis. (Several other types of assistance provided by the national employment fund are paid only in cases of an established or impending unemployment crisis in a specific region or occupation; this assistance is paid under the terms of agreements between the Ministry of Labor and business firms or occupational organizations.)

The decree of April 20, 1964, established the amount for grants and indemnities covering the cost of moving, re-housing, and the transportation of furniture.[4] Workers fulfilling the conditions laid down in the law of December 18, 1963 (Law No. 63-1240), can receive the following grants and indemnities:

Change-of-Location Grants

A grant for change of location (travel) and an indemnity for rehousing are payable to unemployed workers.

A single person who moves less than 100 kilometers from his former place of residence will receive compensation based on his minimum guaranteed wage for 400 hours. (The national minimum guaranteed wage presently fixed at 2. 0075 French francs--$0. 41--in the Paris area; rates are lower in the system's five other wage zones.) If the move is more than 100 kilometers from the former place of residence, the minimum guaranteed wage is for 500 hours. If lodging is necessary at the new place of employment, the minimum interprofessional guaranteed wage is for 800 hours.[5]

A married man with no children who moves less than 100 kilometers from the former place of residence will receive compensation based on his minimum guaranteed wage for 500 hours. If the move is more than 100 kilometers from the former place of residence, the minimum interprofessional guaranteed wage is for 600 hours. If lodging is necessary at the new place of residence, the total minimum interprofessional guaranteed wage is for 1, 000 hours.

A married man with one or two children who moves less than 100 kilometers will receive compensation based on his minimum guaranteed wage for 600 hours. If the distance is more than 100 kilometers, the minimum guaranteed wage is

for 700 hours. If lodging is necessary, the compensation
is on the basis of a minimum guaranteed wage for 1,200
hours.

A married man with three or more children will receive
a minimum guaranteed wage of 700 hours if the move is less
than 100 kilometers from the old residence, and a minimum
guaranteed wage of 800 hours if the move is for more than
100 kilometers. If lodging is necessary, compensation equal
to a minimum guaranteed wage of 2,800 francs is provided.

The change-of-location grant is paid in two equal in-
stallments. The first is paid within one month after arrival
in the new area, and the second is paid at the end of six
months. However, if the worker, after receiving the first
part of the allowance, leaves his employment, he has to return the money he received unless he has been placed in a
new job in a region short of labor. [6]

Travel Allowances

The worker (single or married) can obtain an allowance
for himself and his family equal to the cost of rail transportation from the old to the new residence, based on the
second-class fare on the French railways. Any fare reductions he might have on rail travel (e.g., for a large family)
are taken into consideration.

Moving Allowances

The worker can ask for an indemnity covering the cost
of transporting his furniture from his former residence to
his new residence. This indemnity cannot exceed the cost
of transporting three tons of furniture by the French railways. However, if justification is offered, the amount can
be raised to a limit of 300 francs for one ton of furniture,
450 francs for two tons, and 600 francs for three tons.

The indemnity is paid only if the furniture is transported
within six months after the arrival of the persons involved

in the move.   However, an additional period of time is permitted, provided the party involved is unable to find a home.
This period of time cannot be greater than two years.

The allowances for travel and the removal of furniture
are paid within one month after the arrival of the persons
and the furniture.   Responsibility for payment rests with
the employment office of the Ministry of Labor in the region
to which the move is made.

Grants and allowances permitted under the decree of
April 20, 1964, are for unemployed workers who cannot find
employment in the home area.   They do not apply to farmers
and farm workers.   A separate program for this group is
carried out under the provisions of the decree No. 63-1044
of October 17, 1963.

Relocation of Farmers and Farm Workers

As mentioned earlier, there is a problem of surplus
labor on French farms.   Agricultural population in France
constitutes 20 percent of the adult labor force, compared
with 10 percent in West Germany and 7 percent in the United
States.   Attempts are being made to consolidate the smaller
farms into larger, more efficient operations and to encourage the farm workers to leave the farms and go into
other professions.   Although migration off of the farms has
been heavy, and older farmers have been induced to retire
earlier through pensions (and have been paid an indemnity
for the land), there is still considerable underemployment
of farm labor.   Problem areas include Brittany, the Aquitaine
Basin and Pyrénées, and Bas-Rhone and Languedoc.

In the context of relocation, the objective of French
agricultural policy is to get farmers to leave small farms
in the less efficient areas of France and move to areas where
the agricultural potential is greatest.   France, in essence,
has been divided into two territories based on their suit-
ability for agriculture.   These territories are classified as
"departure" and "reception" zones.   The "reception" zones
include areas with greater agricultural potential and are
usually located around the larger French cities.   Farmers

TABLE 19

Number of French Workers Relocated and Cost
of Relocation, 1960-67

Year	No. of Workers Relocated	Amount in New Francs [1]
1960	340	767,098
1961	752	901,226
1962	1,083	1,670,890
1963	790	1,393,192
1964	1,397	1,465,241
1965	1,505	1,707,343
1966	1,458	1,625,848
1967	1,753	1,907,577

[1] The new franc is worth approximately $.21.

Source: Ministry of Labor; American Embassy.

in the "departure" zones are given financial assistance to take up farming in the "reception" zones. This assistance is also available to farmers in the "departure" zones who wish to secure employment in industry.

Loans and grants are provided to farmers who wish to migrate to the "reception" zones. Funds are available under the social action fund which was created by the Loi Complémentaire of 1962.[7] The social action fund will pay all of the expenses involved in moving to a "reception" area, providing the move is more than 50 kilometers. The expenses include the cost of travel and the removal of furniture and other household effects. In addition, the fund provides a change-of-location grant (settling-in allowance) which varies from 1,250 to 3,000 francs, depending on the region to which the farmer moves.

The provisions above are limited primarily to farmers. Underemployed farmhands who have not had steady employment for at least a year can receive free occupational retraining at a public training center, as well as reimbursement of cost of travel and removal of household effects to the place of training and eventually to the new place of employment.

WEST GERMANY

West Germany has maintained a high rate of economic growth and a low rate of unemployment during most of the postwar period. Exceptions were 1966 and 1967, when a recession occurred, largely through restrictive monetary policies used to cope with an overheating of the German economy in 1965. The growth rate declined from 6.5 percent in 1965 to a postwar low of 1.2 percent in 1967. The rate of unemployment, which had been averaging around 1 percent of the labor force over the period 1960-65, increased to 3.1 percent in the spring of 1967. However, the German economy recovered from the recession in 1968, and the unemployment rate declined to less than 2 percent by the end of the year. It can be said that the German economy is now the most viable in Europe.

Certain areas of Germany have had above-average rates of unemployment. Since 1953, approximately 60 percent of the total number of unemployed workers have lived in the states of Schleswig-Holstein, Lower Saxony, and Bavaria. Unemployment within these states has been concentrated in the areas of Bayrischer Wald, East Friesland, the area around Kassel, and a few areas in southeastern Bavaria. Unemployment also has occurred in the coal mining areas of the Saar and Ruhr, and in the iron ore mines of southern Bavaria. However, unemployment in all of these areas is low by American standards.

In West Germany, redevelopment areas are selected on the basis of the following criteria:

1. Gross per capita production is 50 percent or less of the average for the country.

2. The number of industrial jobs per 1,000 jobs is one-third or less of the national average.

3. Outmigration in excess of 10 departures out of 1,000 inhabitants occurs yearly.

The redevelopment areas include all of Schleswig-Holstein, parts of Lower Saxony, certain agricultural areas along the western frontier, and agricultural areas in Bavaria and North Hesse.

Relocation assistance as a device to stimulate the mobility of unemployed workers is unimportant in West Germany. The overall unemployment rate has been low for most of the decade of the 1960's, and areas with above-average unemployment are not far removed from more prosperous areas. This factor, coupled with the existence of a first-rate transportation system, has meant that companies can locate in just about any area in West Germany and still be close to markets. It also means that most unemployed workers do not have to go far to obtain employment.

Relocation assistance, however, is available to unemployed workers who have no prospect for employment in the home area, and workers who have received notice that they will be dismissed from employment. Subject to a means test, a worker and his family may receive travel expenses, a per diem allowance, an allowance for the removal of furniture and other household effects, a family allowance when housing is not available in the new area (varying inversely with the weekly wage and depending on the distance of separation), and a starting allowance to take care of the family until the worker receives pay on the new job. Allowances of up to 100 Deutsche marks (DM; $25) within any 26-week period may be made to meet the cost of job seeking, and allowances are also available to pay for travel undertaken to take selection tests for a job or a training program.

In West Germany, relocation assistance was of considerable importance in the early 1950's in connection with the resettlement of refugees from eastern Europe. In the 1950's, relocation assistance was used to move unemployed workers from West Berlin to areas in West Germany where employment was available.

Since the erection of the Berlin wall in 1961, a labor shortage has existed in West Berlin, and a reverse movement of workers has occurred. To induce workers to take employment in West Berlin, the Berlin Aid Program provides relocation assistance. This assistance is available to anyone, employed or unemployed, whose skills are needed in West Berlin.

In West Germany, the Federal Office for Placement and Unemployment Insurance and the labor offices of the states are responsible for the implementation of relocation allowances. The federal institution is located in Nuremberg. It is subdivided regionally into 13 regional offices which, in the main, correspond to the states of the Federal Republic, and locally into 210 employment exchanges with 539 branch offices. These cover the entire federal territory, including West Berlin.

The cost of relocation assistance in West Germany has been small. A paramount reason is the means test. Applicants must prove that they do not have sufficient income or other assets to undertake a move. Coal and iron ore miners are eligible for relocation allowances under a separate scheme which is financed by a social fund created by the

European Coal and Steel Community.   Excluding this scheme, the cost of relocation assistance in West Germany between 1960 and 1967 was 25 million DM for travel and removal allowances and 27.4 million DM for starting allowances.

NORWAY

Norway has a low rate of unemployment, currently is around 1.8 percent.   The country has enjoyed economic prosperity over the past decade.   However, regional development has been quite uneven, and unemployment in the fishing and forest industries in northern Norway is above the national average.   (Unemployment during the winter months is at a rate twice the national average.)   Northern Norway has lagged behind the rest of the country from the standpoint of economic growth, and many Norwegians still are tied to marginal farms in the area.   Transportation to the population centers, such as Oslo, is a factor that works to discourage the location of industry in northern Norway.

A considerable decline in employment in farming, forestry, and fishing is anticipated for the Norwegian economy over the next five years.   There has been a decline in employment opportunities in rural areas and an increase in employment opportunity in urban centers.   This also is expected to continue.   For administrative purposes, Norway is divided into 18 rural counties and two city counties--Oslo and Bergen.   During the 10-year period from 1951 to 1960 there was a net emigration from 13 of these counties amounting to 73,000 persons.   The largest number of emigrants came from northern Norway (21,000) and the inland counties of Hedmark and Oppland (19,000).   The counties showing net immigration were Askershus (26,500) and Oslo (22,000).   According to forecasts which have been made, this geographical change will continue.   One factor which may accelerate this development is the continued economic integration of Europe.

Variations in employment opportunities between Norwegian labor market areas have created two major problems:

how to get workers to such areas as Bergen and Oslo, where job vacancies exist; and how to create employment opportunities in areas affected by unemployment and underemployment.

Most manufacturing industries are located in the counties of Oslo and Bergen and the adjacent counties, while the remaining parts of the country are less industrialized and still have a considerable part of their labor engaged in industries with a low level of productivity, mainly agriculture and fishing.

Relocation Assistance

Norway offers several forms of relocation allowances:

1.   Travel allowance. A travel allowance is granted to a person who is unemployed or is likely to be unemployed in the near future, and who through the employment service secures employment in a place where labor is needed. This allowance includes the cost of travel to the new place for an interview and the cost of travel to the new job. Travel reimbursement also is made for journeys to the former place of residence for special reasons--serious illness or death of a close relation, or to visit the family if housing is unattainable at the new place of employment.

A person who has obtained travel allowances may also obtain travel allowances for each member of his family and a removal allowance for furniture and other household goods of up to 1000 kroner. (The kroner is worth $0.14.) The decision to give travel and removal allowances (funded by the unemployment insurance fund) is made by the local employment service. The payment of removal allowances must also be approved by the county employment office.

2.   Family allowance. This allowance (funded by the government) is payable to a worker who has received a travel allowance, provided:

(a) The worker has to maintain two separate households (family housing is not available in the new place of employment);

(b) He is from a labor surplus area; and

(c) He takes employment in a district in which there is a shortage of labor in his industry.

The family allowance lasts for a maximum of 20 weeks. The basic allowance amounts to 360 kroner a month, with an additional six kroner a day for each dependent.

3. Starting allowance. A person who has been granted a travel allowance may also receive a starting allowance (funded by the government) of 400 kroner to help him to his first payday, provided:

(a) He comes from a labor surplus area;

(b) He takes employment in a district where there is a shortage of labor in his industry; and

(c) The work lasts for a minimum of six months.

The granting of the starting allowance is decided by the local employment office after approval from the county employment office.

Cost of Relocation Assistance

In 1965, 22,348 persons received travel and removal allowances amounting to 3,100,000 kroner; 577 family allowances were granted, the expenditure amounting to 300,000 kroner; and starting allowances, amounting to 400,000 kroner, was given to 1,011 persons. (In 1964, 19,000 persons received travel and removal allowances; 300 persons received family allowances; and 500 persons received starting allowances).

In terms of workers moved with relocation assistance relative to the size of the population, Norway ranks second to Sweden. Norway is similar to Sweden in that it is a large country (125, 000 square miles) by European standards, with a sizable length (1, 100 miles) and a small population (3, 700, 000). It is the most sparsely populated of all European countries.

DENMARK

Denmark is a much smaller country than Norway, with a land area of approximately 16, 600 square miles. The population, however, is larger--4, 800, 000 as of 1968.

In Denmark, the geographical areas with problems of structural unemployment consist mainly of sparsely populated regions where agriculture is the main source of employment and where there is relatively little manufacturing industry. Such areas exist in North Jutland, West Jutland, South Jutland, Lolland-Falster, and various small islands. There also is considerable seasonal unemployment, particularly in the building trades. In 1963, unemployment in building and construction varied from 28. 1 percent in February to 1. 6 percent in August.[8]

The Danish government provides loans, guarantees, and grants to local government authorities, private organizations, or individual firms for development of the problem areas. Subsidies also are provided for the development of industrial sites and the construction of sewers and roads in areas earmarked for industry.

Denmark provides travel allowances, removal allowances, family allowances, and housing allowances to unemployed workers who must leave the home area to find employment. This assistance also is available to those workers who are likely to become unemployed in the immediate future.

Travel allowances involve the provision of travel fares and a per diem allowance to cover other costs of traveling.

These allowances are not only for travel when starting work
in the new place of employment, but also for interviews
by the potential employer. As is true in Sweden, the Danish
worker is able to look over the job before accepting or re-
jecting it. Removal allowances to cover the cost of moving
furniture and other household items also are paid to the
worker.

Family allowances are provided to relocated workers for
expenses incurred in maintaining two households. Moreover,
special financial aid in the form of loans is given to the relocatee to purchase a home or to pay rent at the new place of
employment.

In Denmark, travel fares and the per diem allowances
while traveling and removal expenses and family allowances
are paid out of government-approved unemployment funds to
those entitled to the benefits, or out of funds provided by the
public labor exchanges.

HOLLAND

The land area of Holland is 12,616 square miles, and
the population is approximately 11,800,000. The problem in
Holland is not so much one of unemployment as of uneven
economic growth among regions. In some areas there is an
acute shortage of labor.

For the purpose of area redevelopment, Holland is divided into three zones:

1. Development centers, in which economic development must be stimulated, (Criteria for designation as
a development center are decline of employment caused by a
rationalization of agriculture; a surplus of population, resulting in unemployment; and the outmigration of manpower,
resulting in an older population.)

2. Centers which are classified as having too great
a concentration of both population and industry,

3.   Areas in which an economic balance has been achieved.

The country's location and lack of raw materials has led to a heavy concentration of population in western Holland, to engage in shipping and trade. A ring of cities including the three major ones--Amsterdam, Rotterdam, and The Hague--is concentrated in a small area of western Holland. Rapid industrial development has occurred in this area.

In contrast with this well-developed area, several regions, especially in the North and East, have shown a relatively small population increase and a lagging average income, mainly because of the lack of development possibilities in agricultural activities. This problem is the reason an area redevelopment program is designed to improve regional balance.

Relocation assistance is provided to unemployed workers who cannot be expected to find employment in their own area. However, this assistance has been selective, in that only in exceptional cases is it provided to workers moving to the Randstad-Holland area (Amsterdam, Utrecht, Rotterdam, The Hague, and Harlem). More generous allowances are provided to workers who move to development centers than to those moving to other areas. Unmarried workers are not eligible for relocation allowances unless they are disabled.

In Holland, eligible categories of workers for receiving relocation assistance are as follows:

1.   Unemployed persons who cannot find employment in their home area and who are offered employment elsewhere, provided that the new place of employment is not in the congested western part of the country (the Randstad-Holland area);

2.   Unemployed workers who move to areas which are considered development centers under the government's area redevelopment program;

3.   Key employees of manufacturing companies which move from the Randstad-Holland area to development centers;

4.   Disabled unemployed who cannot find employment in the home area and who are offered jobs elsewhere;

5.   Youths up to the age of 21 who wish to take an industrial apprenticeship and who cannot find a suitable company in the home area; and

6.   Unemployed agricultural workers who move temporarily to areas with a shortage of seasonal workers.

Relocation assistance involves travel allowances to enable unemployed workers to search for employment, to key workers involved in industrial decentralization, and to structurally unemployed agricultural workers who move temporarily to labor surplus areas. Financial assistance also is available to commuters, providing that the family cannot be moved to the new place of employment. This assistance is limited to workers who are eligible for relocation assistance, and covers 50 percent of commuting costs for a period of up to one year. Handicapped workers can receive full commuting costs for one year. Lodging and maintenance allowances are paid to unemployed workers while they look for employment. Relocation assistance includes travel allowances for families of unemployed or key workers to cover the cost of moving to the new area, and a removal allowance which covers the cost of moving household possessions. In addition, there is an installation allowance of 300 florins for a married couple, plus 50 florins for each dependent. For a single worker, the installation allowance is 200 florins.

In Holland, relocation assistance discriminates in favor of those workers who move to development centers. Workers moving to areas other than the development centers receive the cost of transportation to the new area, moving expenses, travel expenses to the new area for the worker's dependent, and the lump-sum installation allowance. However, workers moving to development centers receive, in addition to these allowances, 50 percent of the cost of board and lodging or 50 percent of daily commuting expenses for up to a year. On the other hand, unemployed workers moving to the western part of the country are not assisted by relocation allowances unless they are handicapped.

The National Employment Service is responsible for the application of the various relocation assistance measures. It is composed of the state employment office and the state office for additional employment. The state employment office is composed of 86 district offices and 65 local offices.

The cost of relocation assistance in Holland has been minimal. For the period 1960 to 1965, an estimated 755,000 florins ($350,000) were spent on assistance to all categories of workers exclusive of seasonally unemployed agricultural workers. The number of unemployed workers utilizing relocation assistance also is small. This can be explained by the lack of available housing in most of the metropolitan areas in the country; the lack of knowledge of many unemployed workers about the availability of relocation assistance; and the short distances involved in most moves.

BELGIUM

Belgium has an area of 11,779 square miles and a population of 9,600,000. About 16 percent of the population is located in the Brussels area. A language problem exists in the country, and difficulties arise from the political and religious differences between its Flemish and Walloon inhabitants.

Unlike Holland, Belgium started its industrial production on the basis of coal. The development of heavy industry in the regions of Charleroi and Liège has been based on the presence of coal in these areas. Coal mining has been a mixed blessing to the Belgian economy. Although it has formed the base for the development of heavy industry, adjustments in terms of employment have taken place in recent years.

Although the per capita gross national product for Belgium is among the highest in Europe, two problems exist:

1. Regional variations in economic growth and unemployment are considerable in Belgium.[9] Underdeveloped areas, which include declining industries (such as mining,

food, clothing, leather, spinning, earthenware, coke, and
cement), are the provinces of East Flanders, West Flanders,
Luxembourg, and Limburg. Unemployment has been the
highest in West Flanders, East Flanders, and the Louvain
district.

    2.   The rate of unemployment, although low by
American standards, has been higher than the rates for
West Germany, Holland, and France. In 1960, for example,
the unemployment rate in Belgium was 4. 3 percent, as against
0. 9 percent for West Germany, 1. 2 percent for France, and
1. 2 percent for Holland. In 1967, the unemployment rate was
4. 5 percent in Belgium, compared with 2. 2 percent in West
Germany, 2. 3 percent in France, and 2.4 percent in Holland.

    The use of relocation allowances to move unemployed
workers from labor surplus areas is unimportant in Belgium.
The reasons are rather apparent.

    1.   The distance involved in most moves would be
small.

    2.   Belgian area redevelopment policy aims at
stimulating economic development in the less prosperous
areas. Industry is attracted to these areas through the
use of low interest rates, tax exemptions, and the direct
financing of industrial buildings by the Belgian government.
No area in Belgium is far removed from such population
and market centers as Antwerp and Brussels.

    3.   Unemployed coal miners are moved under a
separate program applicable to all Common Market countries.

    The Act of February 14, 1961, gave the Office National
de l'Emploi the responsibility of assisting the relocation of
unemployed workers, and the Royal Decree of March 20,
1961, fixed the amount of relocation assistance available to
unemployed workers. This assistance is not limited to labor
surplus areas.

    Travel and removal allowances are available in Belgium.
However, a worker has to move to a place at least 30 kilometers from his home before he is eligible, or be absent
from his home area, if he is commuting, for at least 12 hours

a day. There is travel assistance available for unemployed
workers to seek employment which amounts to a 75 percent
reduction in railroad fares, and a commuting assistance,
which also involves a reduction in railway fares for a period
of up to a year. There is also a removal allowance which
covers the cost of moving furniture and other household goods,
and an installation allowance which amounts to an average of
three weeks' wages for the worker plus one and one-half
weeks' wages for each dependent, up to a maximum of 12
weeks' wages.

The number of workers receiving relocation assistance
has been very small. In 1966, for example, only 825 workers
received travel allowances, and 5,701 workers received
commuting allowances. Total expenditures over a five-year
period, 1962-66, amounted to 223,000 Belgian francs. (The
Belgian franc is worth $0.02.)

WORKER READAPTATION PROGRAM OF THE
EUROPEAN COAL AND STEEL COMMUNITY

The European Coal and Steel Community was established
in 1952 by the governments of France, the German Federal
Republic, Italy, Belgium, Holland, and Luxembourg as an
administrative agency designed to pool the coal and steel resources of those nations. It subsequently became the nucleus
of the European Economic Community, established by the
same six powers in 1957 to work for a common European
market.

The basic objective of the European Coal and Steel Community was to create a competitive expanding economy in
Europe through the elimination of all tariff barriers (or other
forms of economic discrimination) to the free flow of trade
in coal and steel--products which accounted for 45 percent
of Europe's volume of trade.

The treaty which established the European Coal and
Steel Community created the European Social Fund. The
objective of this fund was to provide better employment

opportunities for coal and steel workers by promoting their
occupational and geographical mobility. Specific aids were
provided for workers whose employment was reduced or
suspended as a result of the elimination of all barriers to the
free flow of trade in coal and steel. (See Article 125 of the
treaty establishing the European Coal and Steel Community.)

It was clear to Robert Schuman, the man most closely
associated with the community, that the successful elimination of tariff and other protective barriers, plus a change-
over to a competitive single market for coal and steel, would
bring with it shifts in production centers, greater productivity
through technical development, and the elimination of marginal
enterprises. These changes would, in turn, lead to unemployment.

The concept of readaptation was developed to meet this
threat. Its aim was to insure that workers did not have to
bear the brunt of the readjustments that had to be made once
the community came into being. Workers who lost employment when a coal mine was shut down would be assisted in
securing employment in another mine, either in the same
area or country, or in one of the other countries in the community. A series of assistance measures which became
known as "readaptation" were provided in the event of unemployment.

Readaptation

Readaptation measures were established in the provisions
which established the European Social Fund. The fund provided assistance for occupational retraining, resettlement
allowances, and compensatory payments to workers whose
employment was temporarily or wholly terminated as a result of closure or conversion of their enterprise to other
production.

Resettlement allowances were contingent upon the unemployed workers' having been obliged to change their residence within the community and upon their having been in
productive employment for at least six months in their new
place of residence.

The European Coal and Steel Community Treaty was amended in 1960 to make readaptation available to all workers affected by radical changes in the demand for coal or steel-- especially workers affected by mine shutdowns. (The amended treaty is known as the Treaty of Paris.) Readaptation provisions then became applicable under Article 56 of the European Coal and Steel Community Treaty. This article provides the current framework within which readaptation is carried out. If the introduction of new technical processes or equipment leads to a large reduction in labor requirements in the coal or steel industries, making it difficult in one or more areas to reemploy the workers discharged, the High Authority of the community can grant nonrepayable assistance as a contribution to the following:

      1.   The payment of compensation to tide the workers over until they can get new employment;

      2.   The granting of resettlement allowances to the workers; and

      3.   The financing of technical retraining for workers who are led to change their employment.

Under the current readaptation program, workers whose jobs have been eliminated can receive the following allowances:

      1.   A tideover allowance between jobs of which there are two kinds--one for discharged workers remaining unemployed, who receive payments on a descending scale; and the other for discharged workers undergoing occupational retraining, who are paid 90 percent of their pre-layoff wages for 12 months;

      2.   A differential allowance, which is paid to men accepting alternative employment at a lower wage than before; under this arrangement, the new wage is made up to 90 percent of the old;

      3.   A resettlement allowance is paid, as a single lump sum, to workers who are obliged to move in order to take a new job; its purpose is to defray expenses incurred in settling elsewhere. This settlement allowance is over

and above the cost of travel for the worker and his dependents and the cost of the removal of furniture and other household effects, both of which are refunded to the worker; and

4.   Free training for a new job.

Two further forms of assistance are given in some countries but not in others:

1.   Reimbursement of daily travel expenses if the worker has to take employment some distance from his home; and

2.   A separation allowance for workers taking a new job which prevents them from returning home daily, thus involving them in additional expense.

Readaptation arrangements are not the same throughout the community. There are some differences in both the tideover and differential allowances from the standpoint of the amount and the length of time for which they are payable and also in the amount of the resettlement grant. In Belgium, the tideover allowance ranges from 10,000 to 12,500 Belgian francs a year; there is no fixed ceiling on wages for which a differential allowance is paid. In France, tideover and differential allowances range from 1,000 to 1,200 French francs a month. In West Germany, tideover and differential allowances range from 750 to 1,000 DM a month; the resettlement allowance is the same for all workers--750 DM for the worker and 250 DM for each dependent, with a maximum of 1,500 DM. The period for which the tideover and differential allowances are available varies from one to two years, depending on the country or part of the country concerned. The cost of readaptation assistance is borne jointly by the country involved and the social fund of the community.

Readaptation Expenditures

More than one coal miner in ten in the six countries of the European Coal and Steel Community has received readaptation assistance since 1954. However, assistance by no means is limited to unemployed coal miners. For

example, from February 1, 1964, to January 31, 1965, out
of 9,437 workers receiving readaptation assistance, 7,616
worked in the coal mines, 759 in the iron mines, and 1,062
in iron smelting. The total number of coal miners receiving
readaptation assistance and the cost of readaptation assistance
are presented in Table 20.

There has been some reluctance on the part of coal
miners to leave their home region. Originally, the community had planned for extensive relocation of coal miners
to the more efficient mines or to related industries. In
France, for example, funds were approved to relocate 5,000
workers from the Centre-Midi region to the Lorraine region,
but only about one-tenth of this number actually moved. As
a result of this reluctance of many workers to move, increased emphasis has been placed on job retraining. Through
the use of inducements, new industries have been encouraged
to locate near the sites of inefficient mines.

Under the European Coal and Steel Community program
for assistance to unemployed workers, member countries
are required to contribute an amount at least equal to that
contributed by the community itself. In exceptional cases,
as in the Belgian Borinage, the Council of Ministers of the
community may by a two-thirds vote, authorize the community to assume all expenditures. Community revenues
are derived from a tax levied directly on coal, steel, and
scrap iron enterprises in the six countries. The amounts
contributed by the countries on a matching basis represent
their sole contribution to the readaptation expenses. West
Germany, France, and Italy, as might be expected, have been
the major contributors. The contributions of Holland and
Luxembourg have been negligible.

Re-Employment of Recipients
of Readaptation Assistance

Very few unemployed coal or iron ore miners have had
to take employment outside of their home country. A general
labor shortage in each of the six countries has resulted in
the reabsorption of the miners into the home economy.

TABLE 20

Expenditures for Readaptation Authorized by the
European Coal and Steel Community, 1954-64

Country	Miners Covered	Expenditures
West Germany	90,112	$24,530,000
Belgium	41,843	13,003,000
France	11,182	4,429,000
Italy	5,330	2,364,000
Total for Community	148,467	44,326,000

Note: Worker readaptation provisions are to be applied to Holland for the first time. The Dutch government plans to utilize readaptation assistance for 27,000 coal miners who will lose their jobs as a result of the partial closure of the Hendrik mine in Limburg. The assistance provided will total $1,380,000.

Source: General Reports on the Activities of the European Coal and Steel Community; and other materials furnished by the community.

Employers try, before laying off workers, to arrange for them to be signed on in another unit of the same company or at another enterprise in the area. In West Germany and Belgium, most of the coal miners discharged have been taken on at other coal mines, usually in the same area. In the Saar, for example, 90 percent of the workers who received readaptation assistance were re-employed in other mines in the area; however, in the Ruhr, only 60 percent were re-employed in other mines.

Unemployed iron ore miners have posed a more difficult problem. As of 1964, employment in the iron ore mines of Germany had at best stabilized, and had worsened in the French mines. Employment is expected to worsen in both countries. Mines are now being closed in southern Germany and in Lorraine. Unemployment in the German mines occurred in Bavaria. A total of 540 workers lost their jobs in 1964. Most were retrained and transferred to jobs within Bavaria. In Lorraine, 400 workers lost employment in the iron ore mines, but most have been reabsorbed in other industries in Lorraine.

Many small mines in the western and Pyrenees ore fields of France have laid off workers. Alternative employment has not often been available, and most miners have to move to other areas to secure employment. This area has few industries and lacks the potential to attract industry. Geographical isolation from major French market centers is a handicap.

SUMMARY

Relocation assistance is provided by other European countries. Austria, Italy, Spain, Ireland, and Finland provide some form of relocation assistance to workers who are unemployed or face the prospect of unemployment in the immediate future. In all countries, the number of workers relocated is small relative to the size of the total labor force.

With the exception of Norway, distance is no barrier to labor mobility. Most unemployed workers can easily find employment in an area within commuting distance of their homes. Continuing high levels of prosperity have increased the ease of obtaining employment. Also, most European countries have a relatively stable labor force. The number of new entrants into the labor force is low for most countries when compared with the United States. This means that there is relatively less pressure on the governments of the European countries to maintain a high rate of economic growth.

Lack of adequate housing is one factor which has probably held down the number of workers who might normally apply for relocation assistance. A shortage of labor and general industrial congestion has encouraged employers to locate in labor surplus areas. Holland has enacted legislation to check the growth of congested areas. Tax inducements and other incentives are used by all European countries to stimulate industrial location in underdeveloped areas.

Reluctance to leave the home area seems to be a deterrent to labor mobility in most European countries. However, this reluctance is limited to older workers with stronger family ties and attachments to the home area. Also, variations in religious and cultural patterns between regions may inhibit mobility, e. g. , Flemish and Walloon regions in Belgium. Reluctance to move also has been noted in connection with the French coal miners in the Centre-Midi coal fields.

It is significant to note, however, that all of the European countries--large and small--do have national programs for relocating unemployed workers. These programs are a part of national manpower policies which are designed to achieve a high rate of employment.

NOTES

1.   Organization for Economic Cooperation and Development (OECD), <u>Problems of Manpower in Agriculture</u>, Report No. 67 (1965), pp. 77-88.

2.   OECD Economic Surveys, France (1967, 1968).

3.   Loi No. 63-1240, Arts. 1, 2.

4.   Also see Decree No. 64-164 (24 Feb., 1964), Art. 3;
Loi No. 63-1240 (18 Dec., 1963).

5.   See Arrêté du 20 Avril, Arts. 3, 7.

6.   Article 3 of Decree No. 64-164 (Feb. 24, 1964).

7.   The two basic laws are Loi d'Orientation Agricole
(1960) and Loi Complémentaire d'Orientation Agricole (1962).
The latter created the Fonds d'Action Sociale pour l'Aménage-
ment des Structures Agricoles.

8.   OECD Manpower and Social Affairs Committee
"Denmark, Reply to Questionnaire No. 10, " Annual Report,
(Paris: OECD, 1964), p. 13.

9.   See U. S. Department of Commerce, Area Redevelopment Administration, Area Redevelopment Policies in Britain
and the Countries of the Common Market, (1965), p. 51.

<table>
<tr><td>CHAPTER</td><td rowspan="3" style="font-size:2em">6</td><td>UNEMPLOYMENT AND
POVERTY IN THE
UNITED STATES</td></tr>
</table>

CHAPTER 6 · UNEMPLOYMENT AND POVERTY IN THE UNITED STATES

INTRODUCTION

At the beginning of the decade of the 1960's, the main economic policy issues in the United States were unemployment and a low rate of economic growth. The unemployment rate was above 6 percent--a rate which compared most unfavorably with unemployment rates in the countries of western Europe. The growth rate also compared unfavorably with growth rates in the Soviet Union and the non-Communist countries of western Europe. During the period from 1951 to 1960, the average annual growth rates of the major industrial countries ranged from 8 percent in Japan to 3 percent in the United States. There was concern that the Soviet Union would provide a formidable economic challenge to the United States if the disparity between the growth rates for the two countries was to continue.

A transformation occurred during the 1960's. The unemployment rate has been reduced well below the interim full employment target of 4 percent set by the Council of Economic Advisers in 1962. The growth rate of gross national product, adjusted for price changes, increased to 6.5 percent a year over the period 1961-67. Poverty superseded unemployment as a basic economic policy issue by 1965. An issue which developed is whether the federal government, by one means or another, should take it upon itself to guarantee that every individual and family in the United States receive a certain level of income each year. By 1968 the sustained success of the economy in terms of growth and full employment was threatened by a rise in prices, and poverty, at least temporarily, had to take a back seat to measures that were designed to reduce the price level.

UNEMPLOYMENT

During the period from 1958 to 1963, the annual rate of unemployment in the United States ranged from a high of 6.8 percent in 1958 to 5.5 percent in 1962. However, unemployment was considerably higher in several areas of the country. Many coal mining counties in Kentucky and West Virginia had unemployment rates in excess of 20 percent for most of this period, and unemployment in general was well above the national average for many other areas within the Appalachian region. Unemployment rates also were high in rural areas of the South and Midwest.

Explanations of the high national unemployment rate centered on two major theoretical approaches--one of which attributed unemployment to a lack of sufficient demand to absorb total national output, and the other of which attributed unemployment to structural changes in the economy. These approaches are called the aggregate demand thesis and the structural transformation thesis,

1.   The aggregate demand theory of unemployment maintains that the total supply of goods produced exceeds the total or aggregate demand necessary to absorb this output. The high unemployment rate of 1958-63, according to this theory, was caused by a deficiency in aggregate demand. Since the principal factor which sets a physical limit to the level of output in any given year is the supply of labor, it is inevitable that any widening of the margin of unused productive potential should be accompanied by an increase in unemployment.

2.   The structural transformation thesis of unemployment argues that the high unemployment rate of the late 1950's and the early 1960's was not caused by a lack of aggregate demand, but by technological change. As the demands of a modern industrial society become more complex, sophisticated machines are created to solve the complexities. As this happens, unskilled and less intelligent workers become unemployed. Directing their attention toward the period from 1957 to 1960, the supporters of the structural transformation thesis reasoned that employment in white-collar and service occupations had increased in

importance while employment in blue-collar and manual occupations had declined. Automation reduced the demand for workers with semi-skilled or unskilled backgrounds. Consequently, this type of worker found it harder to get a job and experienced longer spells of unemployment. [1]

The structural transformation theory is often confused with structural unemployment. Structural unemployment can be defined as a displacement from particular jobs by technological change, or by geographical migration or some other long-run influence. There is somewhat of an obfuscation of the differences between structural transformation and structural unemployment. In essence, the structural transformation thesis stresses the increase and decrease in employment opportunities in different types of occupations --white-collar and service versus blue-collar and manual jobs. Structural unemployment places emphasis on long-run factors and shifts in the relative importance of areas, industries, or occupations.

The different theories call for different economic policies. If unemployment is attributable to a deficiency in aggregate demand, then the appropriate economic policy is to raise the level of total demand. Fiscal policy would be expansive through an increase in government expenditures, or a reduction in taxes, or both. Monetary policy would also be expansive through an increase in the money supply. However, if unemployment is structural in nature, then the appropriate policy prescription would be an increase in the mobility of labor, subsidized movement of unemployed workers out of labor surplus areas, job retraining, and a more effective placement service.

It is necessary to note that these policies are not mutually exclusive. Those who support the aggregate demand thesis agree that the provision of jobs in an expanding economy must be accompanied by job retraining measures to fit workers for these jobs. Programs designed to give aid to depressed areas and to relocate unemployed workers would not be precluded. They say, however, that most of those referred to as structurally unemployed would be quickly employed if job opportunities are plentiful.

The "New Economics"

In the 1960's, traditional concepts of public finance
underwent a major change; government fiscal policies came
to be viewed as instruments for influencing the direction
and magnitude of income flows throughout the economy. The
"new economics" of the Kennedy and Johnson administrations
reflected the belief that economic stability--full employment
without inflation--could be achieved through the use of fine-
tuning adjustments on the country's fiscal and monetary machinery. An example of the "new economics" at work was
the income tax cut of 1964. Its purpose was to assure an
increase in total demand, and hence an increase in the
level of economic activity. Budget policy was also adapted
deliberately in an effort to increase the leval of capital formation. In 1962, the investment credit was introduced with
the purpose of raising the level of investment. It permitted
firms to deduct each year from their tax liability 7 percent
of their investment outlays on equipment. In effect, the
government paid a subsidy on investment by giving back to
firms a fraction of their investment cost through this credit.

In addition to the "new economics" expansionary fiscal
and monetary policies, major programs were developed to
cope with the problem of regional unemployment. One program was established under the provisions of the Appalachian
Redevelopment Act of 1965. The purpose of the act is to develop the infrastructure of the Appalachian region through
the construction of highway facilities and through the expansion of vocational education and farming. The Public
Works and Economic Development Act and its antecedent,
the Area Redevelopment Act, were designed to foster economic development in depressed areas. (In order for an
area to qualify for assistance under the provisions of the
Public Works and Economic Development Act, it must satisfy
at least one of the following criteria: substantial unemployment; persistent unemployment; net outmigration exceeding
25 percent of the population between 1950 and 1960; family
income in 1960 at 40 percent or less of the national median
family income; a major loss in employment opportunities that
will cause unemployment to rise to 50 percent above the
national unemployment rate unless direct action is taken;

an Indian reservation in severe economic distress; or, if
no area in a state qualifies for assistance, that area which
comes closest to satisfying one of the criteria may be eligible
for assistance). Loans and grants are made available for
the construction of public works, and long-term loans at low
interest rates are made available as an inducement to attract
industries into depressed areas. These acts have as their
basic assignment the attraction of jobs to areas of surplus
labor. Their effectiveness in reversing long-term economic
decline is not yet clear. It would appear that outmigration
and the very high level of aggregate demand created by the
Vietnam War have been more important in reducing the level
of unemployment.

To meet the need for job training, the Manpower Development and Training Act was passed in 1962. Its objectives are attuned to the structural transformation thesis.
Priority is given to the provision of job skills to unemployed
workers. Several amendments have broadened the provisions
of the act. In 1963 it was amended to add basic literacy skills
to job training for the unemployed. (The Vocational Education
Act of 1963 has similar objectives.) When high rates of unemployment continued in many regions of the United States,
relocation allowances were written into the law on an experimental basis.

Results of Unemployment Policies

By 1968, the national unemployment rate had declined
to 3.6 percent--the lowest rate since 1953. Part of this reduction can be attributed to the general economic policies
designed to stimulate aggregate demand, and to manpower
and regional development programs. However, a major
reason for the reduction of the unemployment rate to 3.6
percent is the Vietnam War. Much of the increase in aggregate demand has been occasioned by war expenditures.
When the war ends, can the rate of unemployment be kept
down to a level which is consistent with national goals while
some semblance of price stability is maintained?

It is apparent that the maintenance of price stability
and full employment are irreconcilable goals. Although the

unemployment rate has been below 4 percent during 1968
and 1969, inflation has become a major problem. Consumer
prices rose 5 1/2 percent during the period from July, 1968,
to July, 1969--the largest increase since the Second World
War. Since December, 1968, the Federal Reserve System has
pursued a policy of intense restraint on money and credit in
an effort to slow the rate of economic growth and, thereby,
bring inflation under control.

The amount which any economy can produce in the short
run, with existing resources, institutions, and tastes, cannot
exceed certain limits, however great the demand. As unused resources become more fully utilized, there eventually
has to be some sort of a trade-off or compromise between
the goals of full employment and price stability in which part
of one goal is traded for part of the other goal. Otherwise,
if full employment is the prime goal, inflation may well be
the direct consequence. If price stability takes precedence
as the primary goal, then unemployment rates above the desired norm will probably be the logical concomitant. The
desirability of full employment is self-evident. It is a prime
function of an economy to enable everybody willing and able to
work to earn a living. But price stability, too, is a desirable goal of economic policy. Inflation has a deleterious
effect on an economy through changes in income distribution
and through inefficient allocation of resources that eventually
create a loss of output.

In Table 21, unemployment rates and the consumer price
index, which is a measurement of price stability, are compared for the years 1958-68.

It can be seen from this table that a reduction of unemployment below 4 percent has been accomplished by an ac-
celeration of the increase in the consumer price index from
less than 1 1/2 percent a year for the period 1960-65 to
more than 3 percent a year. In the middle of 1969, the unemployment rate was running around 3.8 percent, but the
consumer price index was increasing at a rate which was
well in excess of 5 percent for the year. To reduce the unemployment rate to, say, 3 percent would increase the speed
of inflation. [2] But the problem of balancing unemployment
against price stability is not limited to the United States
alone. Although the western European countries and Japan

TABLE 21

Comparison of Unemployment Rates and Consumer
Prices in the United States, 1958-68

Year	Unemployment Rate	Consumer Price Index
1958	6.8%	100.7
1959	5.5	101.5
1960	5.5	103.1
1961	6.7	104.2
1962	5.5	105.4
1963	5.7	106.7
1964	5.2	108.1
1965	4.5	109.9
1966	3.8	113.1
1967	3.8	116.2
1968	3.6	120.9

Source: Economic Report of the President (1969), pp. 255, 279.

have maintained low unemployment rates through the use of expansionary demand management policies, excess demand has necessitated the taking of stringent policy actions to prevent inflation. The austerity measures taken by the British government to reduce prices and increase exports is a case in point.

It is evident that an appropriate fiscal and monetary policy mix must be developed to maintain some sort of balance between unemployment and price stability. A test of the nation's ability to maintain a high level of employment will come after the end of the Vietnam War and partial demobilization occurs. There should be some decline in defense expenditures which will be counterbalanced in part by built-in increases in budgetary expenditures. The fiscal dividend, which is the difference between an increase in federal revenues occasioned by a rising gross national product and increases in government expenditures, should be increased by a decrease in defense spending. The dividend can be used in two ways: distribution to consumers in the form of lower taxes or for use in major new government programs involving income maintenance and aid to the cities.

GEOGRAPHICAL DISTRIBUTION
OF UNEMPLOYMENT

Unemployment is unevenly distributed throughout the United States. In 1968, the national unemployment rate for the nation was 3.6 percent. But that does not tell us anything about geographic variations in unemployment. First, there is a significant difference in unemployment by major geographic regions for 1968. In the Northeast region (New England and Middle Atlantic), the unemployment rate was 3.2 percent; in the North Central region (East North, North, and West North), the rate was 3.0 percent; in the South (Atlantic, East South Central, and West South Central), the rate was 3.7 percent; and in the West (Mountain and Pacific), the rate was 4.9 percent. [3]

When the major regions are further broken down on a state basis, variations in unemployment continue to exist to

a considerable degree.   Unemployment rates for the ten
largest states, which together contained 45 percent of all
workers in 1968, show even wider variations than the regional
rates.   Table 22 ranks these states according to their 1968
average unemployment rates.

There are variations in unemployment within a state.
In 1968, the average unemployment rate for the state of Virginia was 2. 8 percent, compared with the national average of
3. 6 percent.   However, the unemployment rate for Dicken-
son County was 7. 0 percent; Lee County, 10. 2 percent; Scott
County, 9. 2 percent; and Wise County, 9. 5 percent.   Several
other Virginia counties had unemployment rates in excess of
6 percent.   The point to be made is that while fiscal and
monetary policies can be used to raise the level of aggregate
demand to a point at which a national rate of unemployment
is at a desired level consistent with full employment goals,
their impact is uneven on regions.

West Virginia offers a similar case in point.   In December, 1968, the unemployment rate for the state was 5. 7
percent, compared with the national rate of 3. 6 percent.
The unemployment rate for eleven counties was in excess of
10 percent.   Taylor County had an unemployment rate of
17. 5 percent, and Webster County had an unemployment rate
of 14. 3 percent.   Other counties with high unemployment
rates were Braxton County, 13. 4 percent; Calhoun County,
12. 5 percent; Lincoln County, 11. 6 percent; Randolph County,
12. 5 percent; Tucker County, 11. 7 percent; and Mason County,
10. 2 percent.   Greenbrier and Monroe counties had a combined unemployment rate of 10. 9 percent, and Mingo and Mc
Dowell counties, in the heart of the coal mining area of the
state, had unemployment rates of 9. 8 and 8. 8 percent. [4]
Although the state and county unemployment rates were affected to some extent by seasonal factors, there was little
variation in the rates in comparison with the average unemployment rates for the year.   By any criterion, the unemployment rates in many West Virginia counties remained
high during a period when the national unemployment rate
was at its lowest point in nearly 20 years.

In Kentucky, variations in unemployment among counties
is quite pronounced.   The average unemployment rate for
the state in 1968 was 4. 1 percent.   Unemployment rates

TABLE 22

Average Unemployment Rates in the Ten
Largest States, 1968

State	Unemployment Rate
California	5.1%
Michigan	3.9
Florida	3.8
Pennsylvania	3.4
Texas	3.4
Ohio	3.4
New Jersey	3.3
New York	3.1
Illinois	2.9
Massachusetts	2.9
U.S. unemployment rate	3.6

Source: Paul M. Schwab, "Unemployment in the ten Largest States and Major Regions,"
Employment and Earnings and Monthly Report on the Labor Force (May, 1969).

ranged from a low of 1.1 percent in Boone County to 25 percent in Owsley County. A number of other counties had high unemployment rates. Leslie County had an average unemployment rate for 1968 of 22.7 percent. Knott County had an unemployment rate of 20.4 percent, and Martin County had a rate of 20.0 percent. [5] Other counties with unemployment rates in excess of 14 percent for 1968 were Bell, Breathitt, Edmondson, Elliott, Estill, Knox, Lyon, Magoffin, and Wayne. Out of a total of 120 Kentucky counties, 29 had an average unemployment rate of 10 percent or more for 1968. Moreover, there was little change in unemployment rates in many counties over preceding years. In 1965, 31 Kentucky counties had unemployment rates in excess of 10 percent-- two more than in 1968. Even though the national rate of unemployment was below 4 percent for 1967 and 1968, a number of Kentucky counties continued to maintain unemployment rates four to five times the national average.

High unemployment rates in both West Virginia and Kentucky are confined primarily to coal mining areas where employment opportunities have decreased. High unemployment rates, however, are not limited to coal mining areas. In October, 1967, the unemployment rate in five farming counties in the rich Delta areas of Mississippi was 7.5 percent. Washington County had an unemployment rate of 9 percent. The average unemployment rate for 1967 was estimated to be in excess of 10 percent for the five counties. This rate does not include the underemployed workers, or those workers who had dropped out of the labor force. When these groups are included, the number of workers either unemployed or underemployed was in excess of 25 percent of the total labor force in these five rural Mississippi counties. [6] This tends to illustrate the fact that the potentially available supply of labor in rural areas is often substantially higher than crude unemployment statistics would indicate.

California, a major industrial state, also affords a contrast in terms of variations in unemployment rates by labor market areas. In 1968, the unemployment rate for the state ranged from a high of 5.7 percent in February to a low of 3.6 percent in October. The unemployment rate in labor market areas in the eastern part of the state was considerably higher than the state average. Variations in seasonal unemployment were significant, reflecting the fact

that much of the eastern part of California is a farming area.
The unemployment rate in the Fresno labor market area
ranged from a high of 9.6 percent in February to a low of
3.5 percent in October. The average rate for the year was
6.8 percent. In the Stockton labor market area, the seasonally
adjusted unemployment rates ranged from a high of 7.2 percent to a low of 5.6 percent for the year, and the average rate
for the year was 6.6 percent. [7]

Several smaller labor market areas had unemployment
rates in excess of 10 percent for 1968. Nevada County had
an unemployment rate of 10.5 percent. The highest rate was
18.8 percent in February and the lowest rate was 5.6 percent in September. Butte County had an annual average unemployment rate of 10.9 percent--compared with 11.1 percent for the same county in 1961. San Benito County had an
average rate of 11.4 percent for the year. The highest rate
was 22.2 percent for February and the lowest rate was 4.0
percent for September. El Dorado County had an average rate
of 10.9 percent, and Shasta County had an average rate of
10.4 percent. Merced, Stanislaus, and Tuolumne counties
had unemployment rates of 9.6, 9.1, and 9.9 percent, respectively. Imperial County had an unemployment rate of
8.2 percent for the year, with very little monthly variation.

California unemployment rates reflect the fact that a
substantial fraction of unemployment in the United States is
the result of seasonal unemployment in industry and agriculture. In agriculture, the seasonal swings can be substantial. From a midwinter low in employment in January
to a midsummer peak in June, there is an increase of approximately 1.1 million agricultural jobs--an expansion of
almost one-third of the total agricultural labor force. [8] In
the second half of the year, there is a sharp decline in employment. However, the peak in overall unemployment for
the nation is not in midwinter, when it might be expected, but
in June when agricultural employment is at its peak. Actually,
agriculture and agriculture-related industries furnish substantial summer employment to students seeking vacation
work and to women who are occasional or intermittent workers,
but not enough to match the increased labor supply at this
time of year.

To dig still more deeply into the problem of local areas of unemployment, in 1966 the Bureau of Labor Statistics began a series of surveys of employment conditions in urban poverty neighborhoods. In 1968, it published a comprehensive analysis of the unemployment problems of the poorest one-fifth of the neighborhoods in the 100 largest metropolitan areas. These poverty neighborhoods were found to contain an extremely high percentage of Negroes. All classes of workers living in poverty neighborhoods have abnormally high rates of unemployment. For the whole group, the unemployment rate was 6. 8 percent in 1967, as against 3. 4 percent for workers living in other neighborhoods. Furthermore, almost one-quarter of the teenagers were unemployed, a rate that is nearly double the teenagers' rate in other urban neighborhoods.

Regional variations in unemployment can be expected to continue. Even though national unemployment rates are maintained at a low rate, labor market imperfections create areas of labor surpluses. An active manpower policy is necessary to reduce the conflict between price stability and full employment. In part, this policy can create additional supplies of needed labor from the ranks of the underemployed and unemployed. Increasing the occupational and geographical mobility of labor in this manner involves both increasing the range of desirable opportunities for the underemployed or unemployed worker and reducing the cost and risk of movement. The components of an effective program to induce more and better-directed labor mobility can be divided into three categories:

     1.   Knowledge of the availability of new jobs under equivalent or superior terms of employment;

     2.   Adequate training for such jobs; and

     3.   The preservation or supplementation of accumulated assets and the maintenance of income during the transition period.

POVERTY

Poverty is related to the problem of unemployment. However, there are several million people who hold low-paying jobs which, even at full-time, full-year employment pay too little to raise them above the poverty level. A preliminary estimate indicated that in 1968, 22 million Americans lived in households with incomes below a defined level of poverty. [9] The gains made in economic growth in recent years have not benefited all parts of the country equally, for there are pockets of poverty which have scarcely been affected. These pockets are found mainly in rural areas, including Indian reservations, and in the inner city, where low-income persons, particularly minority groups, reside.

Definitions of poverty are at best arbitrary. In general, poverty is said to occur when a family or an individual does not have sufficient income to provide for a socially defined minimum standard of living. This standard is based on estimates of the realistically minimal costs of providing food, clothing, shelter, and health services for adults and children. The official count of the poor is based on annual income. A four-person, non-farm family is considered poor if its income is less than $3,335 at 1966 prices of consumer goods. For a seven-person, non-farm family, the poverty line is $5,430. Because farm families have less need for cash income, they are not considered poor if their incomes exceed 70 percent of the non-farm standards. This means that a four-person farm family would need a minimum annual income of $2,345 a year. Minimal incomes for individuals are $1,635 for a non-farm individual and $1,145 for a single person who lives on a farm.

A "near poverty" indicator has been developed by the Social Security Administration. This standard is set at incomes averaging one-third higher than the poverty line of income but less than one-half of median family income. For example, for a non-farm family of four, the "near poverty" income line is $4,345 a year. For a family with seven members or more, the "near poverty" income line is $6,945. For farm families, the "near poverty" income line is less--$3,060 a year for a family with four or more persons, and $4,850 a year for a

family with seven or more persons. The "near poverty"
income line is $1, 945 for non-farm individuals and $1, 390
for farm individuals. 10

The poor cannot be lumped into a homogeneous group.
In 1966, there were 29. 7 million poor persons in the United
States, according to a survey made by the Bureau of the Census.
This total included 12. 5 million children under the age of 18
living in poor families, and 5. 4 million elderly persons aged
65 and over. The remainder of the poor consisted of 2. 1
million adults who lived alone, 4. 6 million family heads, and
5. 1 million wives and other family members.

Poverty is not confined to any single geographic area,
but exists to the greatest extent in the rural areas of the
South and the Appalachian region. There is also a considerable amount of poverty in the ghettos in the major central
cities in the United States. Although a greater percentage of
Negroes relative to whites are classified as poor, 71 percent
of all poor families and 83 percent of unrelated individuals
are white according to 1967 data.

In September, 1967, the National Advisory Commission
on Rural Poverty completed a year-long study of rural
poverty and submitted it to the White House. 11 The study
reflected concern over poor rural environmental conditions
which have caused an exodus of thousands of rural Americans
--both Negro and white--to urban areas throughout the United
States. Usually lacking requisite job skills, a number of
these people have remained unemployed, and countless others
have gone on relief, thus compounding already complex urban
problems. This unprecedented exodus is expected to continue,
with a resultant decline in the rural population and an aggravation of urban problems, unless remedial steps are taken
to halt or reverse the rural to urban population movement.

In its report, The People Left Behind, the National Advisory Commission states:

"It is a shocking fact that in the United States today,
in what is the richest nation in history, close to 14 million rural Americans are poor, and a high percentage of
them are destitute. "

The measure of poverty was taken as an average family income of $3,000 or less a year. Although low income is used as the basic index of poverty, lack of job opportunities, proper housing, schooling, and health services are also tangible indices. The commission noted that the mass exodus from rural areas has changed the population composition in favor of the less productive and viable segments--the aged and the young. In many low-income households, the head is often 65 years of age or older.

The commission found that although only 30 percent of the nation's population is in rural areas, 40 percent of the nation's poor live there. The total rural poor includes 3 million families and a million unattached persons. There was not only a higher percentage of poor people in rural areas, but the level of poverty was more extreme. An income of $3,000 in rural areas was an exception rather than the rule. It was found that more than 70 percent of the poor families in rural America have less than $2,000 a year income, and one family out of four exists on less than $1,000 a year.

The commission also found that, contrary to popular impression, all the rural poor do not live on farms, nor are all of them Negroes. Most live in small towns and villages. Only one in four of the rural poor families live on a farm, and out of 14 million poor people in rural areas, 11 million are white.

The Economic Research Division of the U.S. Department of Agriculture estimated that about 800,000 rural adults between the ages of 20 and 64 were unemployed in 1960. This analysis also estimated the significance of underemployment in rural areas. It was found that, on the average, persons employed in rural areas were 18 percent underemployed. For rural farm residents, the rate of underemployment was about 37 percent.

Prominent among the factors responsible for rural poverty is the rapid technological development in agriculture. Development of labor-saving machinery, minimum tillage methods of cultivation, and herbicides have resulted in a reduction in the demand for labor in agriculture. Similar changes have occurred in other natural resource-based industries in rural America. These technological changes

have forced the people displaced to seek employment elsewhere. Often these people have been poorly equipped for other
occupations. At the same time, the employment opportunities
in the small towns serving rural America also have suffered
as changes in transportation and communication have made it
possible for people to look to the larger cities for business
services.

Since the demand for agricultural products is highly in-
elastic and increasing relatively slowly, the technological
developments in agriculture have been such as to require
the shift of resources to other uses. The resource involved
in most cases is the human resource. As the derived demand
for farm labor has declined, those who are displaced are
faced with three alternatives: unemployment, underemployment, or movement into non-farm employment.

A force at work in the rural areas is that of underemployment. It is generally related to the technological development in agriculture and under-investment in human resources. Much of the underemployment in rural areas can
be attributed to inadequate monetary and fiscal policies of the
federal government, imperfections in the labor market, and
lack of economic development in rural areas. However, the
point has been made that monetary and fiscal policies have an
uneven impact on regions. Although their effect on the national economy may be to maintain a level of aggregate demand consistent with a high level of employment, the spill-
over effect on rural areas may be negligible. As for the
lack of economic development, admittedly there is a need to
bring jobs into rural areas. But how can jobs be created
and how can private capital be stimulated to flow into rural
areas?

A solution which has been proposed is to use tax incentives, for given large enough incentives, most locations can
be made attractive to industry. However, it is also necessary
to provide various facilities and services in rural areas.
Educational facilities have to be improved, and more emphasis has to be placed on vocational training. A major facet
of the problem in rural areas stems from the fact that education and training of the people in these areas is out of step
with existing economic opportunities. Unless rural youth

are trained for the types of jobs which exist today and which
will emerge tomorrow, they are destined to join the ranks of
the unemployed.

Tax incentives take a variety of forms, including accelerated depreciation, investment credits, exemptions
from property taxes, exemptions from income taxation to
stimulate savings, and special deductions and exemptions--
such as exemption of exports from taxation. France, for
example, exempts all exports from the value-added tax. West
Germany, probably more than any other country, has had
spectacular success in using tax incentives to stimulate economic growth, as well as recovery and reconstruction of the
economy after the end of the Second World War.

One of the difficulties in evaluating inducements designed
to attract industry is the number of factors which bear on the
final decision to locate an enterprise. Actually, tax incentives
would be one of many factors, which include access to markets,
availability and cost of labor, availability of raw materials,
transportation costs, water and fuel supplies, and the quality
of public services. The importance of the tax incentive would
vary between industries, with capital-intensive industries regarding it as more important than labor-intensive industries.
For example, the current 7 percent investment credit has
meant more to the capital-intensive airline industry than to
the labor-intensive textile industry.

In January, 1969, the Rural Job Development Act (S. 15)
was introduced by Senator Fred Harris, Democrat from
Oklahoma, and Senator James Pearson, Republican from
Kansas. Its general purpose is to give tax benefits to business firms that invest in rural areas. The principle tax
benefits are:

1. A tax credit of 7 percent on investments made in
depreciable real property;

2. A tax credit of 14 percent on investments made
in depreciable personal property;

3. An accelerated depreciation of two-thirds the
normal, useful, or class life for machinery, equipment, and
buildings; and

4.   A deduction of 125 percent for salaries and wages paid to workers for a period of three years.

These incentives would be available only to firms that locate or expand operations in rural areas designated by the Department of Agriculture. A firm would have to meet certain employment standards. The more important standards are that the new or expanded facility must result in the full-time employment of at least 10 additional persons from the rural area, and that at least 50 percent of the persons employed must reside in or near the facility. If the required employment standards are not maintained, the tax incentives can be eliminated or recaptured.

President Nixon has given tax incentives high priority in terms of their application to the solution of social problems. They are to be used to provide job opportunities and housing in urban poverty areas as well as to provide job opportunities in rural areas. The rationale for their use is the involvement of private enterprise in solving national problems. There is impatience on the part of many groups with the inability of the federal government to solve some of these problems directly. Undoubtedly, a major impetus for the use of tax incentives is the generally high marginal tax rates that have prevailed in the United States since the end of the Second World War. Why not harness all the energies that go into avoiding these high rates to socially desirable goals?

There is evidence to suggest that the Rural Job Development Act could have some effect on plant location. For example, the Office of Defense Mobilization provided special depreciation provisions to firms locating in labor surplus areas during the Korean War. These provisions became effective in November, 1953, and certificates were issued by the Office of Defense Mobilization to 74 firms during the period from 1953 to 1959. These certificates represented an investment of $320 million, but accounted for only one-tenth of 1 percent of the total cost of all facilities that were certified for accelerated depreciation during the Korean and post-Korean War periods. The Office of Defense Mobilization estimated that more than 17,000 jobs were created in labor surplus areas under the 74 certificates.

Available evidence concerning similar approaches used by other countries indicates that tax incentives do have some effect on industrial location. Free depreciation was permitted firms locating in British development areas, and a number of American and British firms took advantage of this incentive to build plants in designated areas in Wales, northern England, Scotland, and Northern Ireland. However, there were also a number of other incentives which were available under provisions of the local Employment Act of 1962 that must be taken into consideration. Moreover, the geographical area involved is smaller than the eastern half of Kentucky.

Presumably, the same criticism could be leveled at the use of investment tax credits and accelerated depreciation to attract industry to rural areas that is leveled against all inducements, namely, that they promote the growth of marginal enterprises having poor working conditions and wages so low that employee earnings are still near the poverty level. However, it seems extremely doubtful that a marginal enterprise, such as a garment factory, would be in a position to utilize an investment credit, for it would have little in the way of capital investment. Moreover, it would be an easy task to utilize a screening technique to eliminate the marginal firm from consideration for the tax incentive.

Another objection to the use of the tax structure for aiding problem areas is that such use constitutes undesirable tinkering with the tax structure and results in damage to the equity and efficiency of the federal tax system. In general, there has been opposition to the use by the Treasury of incentives to solve social problems, on the grounds that it involves a form of "back door" financing which is much more difficult to control than regular government expenditures. Put simply, tax incentives, if extended to every social problem, would erode the base of the corporate income tax, which is one of the major sources of tax revenue. Proponents of this viewpoint argue that if assistance is to be given to new or expanding firms in rural areas, it should be done through the use of direct subsidies, such as grants, rather than through indirect tax devices. At least, in this way, the Treasury and Congress can maintain some direct control over the use of subsidies.

From the standpoint of tax equity, it has been contended that the tax system would be used to discriminate between

locations and firms. The argument takes the following line
of reasoning: Firm A locates in a healthy economic area, and
does not receive special tax treatment. Firm B, on the other
hand, locates in an economically depressed area, thus qualify-
ing for special investment credit and depreciation benefits.
Firm A thus pays a higher tax than Firm B and, in essence,
subsidizes Firm B, which may be its competitor. Moreover,
the tax incentive may have the effect of diverting capital from
more efficient to less efficient uses.

However, it can also be argued that Firm B, by locating
in a higher-risk area in an effort to reduce economic inequal-
ity between urban and rural areas, is entitled to special treatment. Moreover, the tax incentive may accomplish the desired objective of stimulating economic development, thus
compensating for the loss of tax equity and revenue which results from differential use of the investment credit. If employment is created as a result of investment incentives, proponents contend, increased income would serve to counterbalance the loss of tax revenue which would occur when the
investment credit is granted.

One problem involving the use of any tax incentive is the
development of standards that would govern its use. The Rural
Job Development Act, for example, is extremely broad in its
application, and a large number of rural counties would be
eligible for assistance, including counties that are relatively
wealthy. This could mean that the tax incentives offered by
the act would attract industry to wealthier rural areas, or
counties contiguous to industrial areas, while the less wealthy
rural areas receive little or no benefit. Thus, the poorer
counties would continue to be frustrated in their attempts to
develop employment opportunities.

The most important question that can be raised in connection with the use of tax incentives is whether they will be effective in accomplishing desired employment goals. There are
two important issues involved. First of all, will tax incentives
have much of an impact on industrial location? Second, when
a plant actually does locate in a depressed area, who will be
employed? The answer to the first question is difficult. It
would depend to a certain extent on the type of industry involved.
A capital-intensive industry would be more likely to utilize the
investment credit than a labor-intensive industry, as evidenced

by the fact that the major users of the credit have been the
airline and steel industries. It is also necessary that tax costs
represent a small part of the total cost of a business firm.
Would the savings in tax costs from the use of tax incentives
be more than counterbalanced by an increase in other costs in
rural or depressed areas? The answer is that in many, if not
most, situations, they would. It can be said that tax incentives
might have a marginal effect in cases where other cost differentials between areas are small.

When an industry is established in a rural or depressed
area, employment opportunities may or may not open up for
local workers. If the industry is capital-intensive, employment may be available only for skilled workers. But if the
local unemployed workers do not possess the requisite job
skills--which is likely--there will be few employment opportunities available. This would mean, of course, that the industry would bring in most of its workers from outside areas,
thus leaving the local unemployed unaffected. Although additional peripheral jobs are created by the location of an industry,
they may well be in the service or professional category.

This point is substantiated by a case study of the employment effects that a large industry had when it located in a depressed area. [12] In 1956, an aluminum reduction and rolling
mill was built by the Kaiser Aluminum and Chemical Company
at Ravenswood, West Virginia, a small town located in an
agricultural area of the state. A decline in agricultural activities had caused a general outmigration from the area. As the
Kaiser plant went into operation, an effort was made to give
first hiring priority to workers from the Ravenswood area.
This proved unsuccessful, for it was discovered that the local
workers did not possess the requisite job skills. Even though
standards were relaxed, the qualifications of most of the unemployed and underemployed workers fell far short of those
necessary to obtain employment. Most of the workers had to
be imported from areas outside the state. As the plant increased its operation, skill requirements also increased, and
unskilled workers were gradually replaced.

The Kaiser workers were not drawn from the ranks of the
local unemployed or underemployed. Although some 4,000
workers were employed at the plant, only 400 to 500 of them
came from the local area. [13] Some of these had moved from

the area, had acquired skills, and had returned home when the plant started operations. Moreover, the secondary effects on employment were also disappointing. Although a number of additional jobs were created in Ravenswood, those that required any degree of skill also were filled by outsiders. Some low-skilled jobs opened up in service stations and retail stores.

New industry in rural area cannot solve unemployment problems unless local workers are trained to handle the new jobs which will be created. To a certain extent, this problem can be remedied through the provision of training programs and training allowances for low-income individuals in rural areas. (The Rural Job Development Act contains provisions for job training programs in rural areas.) However, when rural areas are defined, they include more than a third of the land area of the United States. It is to be seriously doubted that all of this area can be covered with industry regardless of the extent of tax incentives.

MANPOWER POLICY

Along with fiscal and monetary policies designed to maintain high levels of employment and business activity, there is a need for more specialized and selective measures which would create jobs in labor surplus areas and encourage the flow of manpower from such areas to expanding and productive industries. Although fiscal and monetary policies can reduce the national rate of unemployment, eventually a point is reached where a trade-off has to occur between the goals of full employment and price stability. How much of a trade-off depends on the national importance of each goal. Moreover, it has become increasingly obvious that fiscal and monetary policies are blunt instruments which can produce an uneven effect on all sectors of economic activity. Such effects may be difficult to control. Also, all sectors of an economy are not ordinarily equally in need of stimulating or braking; nor do they require such action at the same time. A point that has been repeatedly made throughout this study is that although general demand-generating fiscal and monetary devices have succeeded in maintaining low national rates of unemployment in all major industrial countries, pockets of high unemployment continue to defy the use of these measures.

By promoting the mutual adjustment of manpower needs and resources, an active manpower policy has the special advantage of being expansionary with respect to employment and production, but anti-inflationary with regard to costs and prices. In fact, an effective manpower policy, by increasing the skills and productivity of the labor force, can help to increase the rate of economic growth and to reduce the level at which a trade-off between the full employment and price stability goals has to occur. So the point is this: General demand-producing fiscal and monetary measures may be expected to keep the national unemployment rate in the United States at or below 4 percent. But manpower policy measures, used selectively in those areas where they are needed, can be expected to reduce the rate of regional unemployment, and hence the national unemployment rate.

A successful manpower policy includes a number of activities which bridge both the supply and the demand side of the labor market. One solution to the social and economic problems of unemployment is the retraining and education of those who are without jobs. Where present skills possessed by workers are inadequate to equip them for a job, manpower policy would be concerned with providing new skills through retraining. Where mobility is limited by an inability to pay the costs of movement, there may be a provision of various kinds of maintenance, removal, family, and starting allowances. Improvement of both the occupational and the geographical mobility of the labor force has to be an important part of any effective manpower policy.

Manpower policy also involves the creation of employment opportunities for disadvantaged groups. For example, the Neighborhood Youth Corps in-school program enables poor youths to earn money and stay in school. The jobs performed by Neighborhood Youth Corps enrollees normally require minimum skills. Although the corps offers needed income to poor youths, it adds little to employability, a fact which suggests that a substantial training component should be added to the program. There is also the Job Corps, which differs radically from the Neighborhood Youth Corps in that it attempts to take disadvantaged youths and equip them with marketable skills as well as to provide them with a basic education. To accomplish this objective, Job Corps centers were created throughout the country. Both the Job Corps and the Neighborhood

Youth Corps were created under the provisions of the Economic
Opportunity Act of 1964. This act was designed to combat
poverty and unemployment and to foster equality of opportunity
by promoting investment in the education, training, and skills
of the poor so that they can contribute more effectively to
society and improve their earning ability.

The most important training programs for unemployed
and underemployed workers are those which have been developed
under the Manpower Development and Training Act of 1962.
Expenditures for training and work-training programs have
increased from $50 million in 1963, which was the first year
in which the act was in operation, to $407 million in 1968. [14]
In 1969, an estimated 275,000 workers will receive some form
of job training under the provisions of the act. This training
includes basic education and employment orientation as well
as the learning of job skills, and is oriented to a major degree
toward minority groups, the long-term unemployed, older
workers, and teenagers. Training can be divided into two
categories -- institutional training and on-the-job training.
The latter is designed to provide part-time training that will
upgrade the employment skills of workers who possess lower-
skilled jobs. This is also supposed to open up employment
opportunities for disadvantaged workers.

Through the Job Opportunities in the Business Sector
(JOBS) program sponsored by the National Alliance of Business-
men, nearly 12,000 cooperating business firms have helped
disadvantaged workers find employment. The premise of the
program is that the best job training is a job. The federal
government is supposed to locate the unemployed and place
them, and business firms are supposed to train them and provide them with jobs. Any extra cost involved in training the
hard-core unemployed is paid by the federal government. In
1969, an estimated 140,000 workers are to receive employment
under the JOBS program.

On August 12, 1969, President Nixon sent a new Manpower
Training Act to Congress. The act proposes to consolidate
major manpower development programs administered by the
Department of Labor -- namely, the Manpower Development
and Training Act and Title 1-A (Job Corps) and 1-B (Community
Work and Training Program) of the Economic Opportunity Act.
These programs, to be operated in conjunction with strengthened

state manpower agencies, are supposed to provide training activities in a cohesive manpower system.   The Office of Economic Opportunity, without major manpower responsibilities, is supposed to continue its role in research work and program development.

Decentralization of administration of manpower services to the states is to occur.   This is to take place in three stages. First, a state will administer 25 percent of the funds apportioned to it when it develops a comprehensive manpower planning capability; second, it will exercise discretion over two-thirds of the funds when it establishes a comprehensive manpower training agency; and third, it will administer 100 percent of the funds when it meets objective standards of performance in planning and carrying out its manpower service system.

As an incentive to move from welfare rolls to payrolls, the allowance to welfare recipients who go into training would be increased $30 per month above their present welfare benefits.   As the welfare recipient moves up the ladder from training to work, the first $60 a month would not be deducted from federally financed payments.

Probably the most important aspect of the proposed Manpower Training Act would be the creation of a national computerized job bank which would match job seekers with job vacancies.   It would operate in each state, with regional and national activities undertaken by the Secretary of Labor.   The computers of the job bank would be programmed with data on job opportunities.   A job seeker would tell an employment counselor his employment background and his skills, which would be matched with available job openings.

The manpower training system would also be designed to act as an automatic stabilizer.   When an increase in unemployment portends a downturn in economic activity, countercyclical manpower programs would be provided.   An increase of 10 percent in appropriations for manpower services would be made if the national unemployment rate equaled or exceeded 4. 5 percent for three consecutive months.   Those who are unemployed could use this time to improve their job skills.

The Nixon manpower program is a part of the "New Federalism, " the name of a new domestic program which also is designed to institute revenue-sharing with state and local governments and to reform the welfare system. The major component of the "New Federalism" would be a $4 billion welfare system with a minimum annual payment of $1,600 for needy families. This plan is to cover the working poor as well as those with no incomes, and would require unemployed adult recipients to obtain job training or employment to receive benefits.

SUMMARY

The United States has maintained an unemployment rate of less than 4 percent since 1966--an exceptional performance when compared with unemployment rates during the 1958-64 period. This success can be attributed to a high level of aggregate demand occasioned in part by increased expenditures in Vietnam, and to various manpower measures which were adopted by the Kennedy and Johnson administrations. However, a rise in the price level has to some extent counterbalanced the success in reducing the unemployment rate, and current economic policy is concerned with inflation rather than unemployment. Implicit in this policy is the recognition that some sort of trade-off between a higher unemployment rate and a lower rise in prices is inevitable.

Even though the national unemployment rate is below 4 percent, there are certain local market areas with unemployment rates which are several times the national average. The point has been made that even in countries such as Sweden and the United Kingdom, where national rates of unemployment have been at a low level for two decades, high unemployment rates in certain areas continue to exist. This phenomenon is relevant to other European countries and to Canada as well. It is important to note that the average unemployment rates in some rather diverse local labor market areas have been in excess of 10 percent or more for the decade of the 1960's, despite national policies to stimulate aggregate demand and to encourage the flow of capital into these areas. It would appear that high unemployment rates in many of these areas can be attributed to imperfections in the labor market, and need to be remedied by selective rather than general measures. Area labor surpluses will remain even after a nationally tolerable rate of unemployment is taken for granted, and the only realistic hope for many unemployed in these areas is to secure gainful employment through relocation. The acquisition of useful skills through retraining will make such relocation possible.

As the problem of unemployment has begun to recede in national importance, another problem -- that of poverty -- has come to the fore and begun to occupy public attention. Although there is an interrelationship between unemployment and poverty, the latter is by no means limited to those persons who are unemployed. Instead, it is spread across a number of groups -- the unemployed and underemployed, the aged, families headed by a woman, and unskilled workers who fail to earn enough to place above the poverty level. As poverty has assumed a national priority, a number of programs have been developed, most of them centered in the Office of Economic Opportunity. Many of these programs attempt either to provide jobs skills or to create some form of employment opportunity for workers.

The Nixon administration has proposed measures which are supposed to represent a radical departure from existing programs in public welfare and manpower training. In public welfare, a modified form of a guaranteed income for families who cannot adequately support themselves and their children is proposed. Minimum welfare payments are to be set for each state by establishing a federally financed income floor.

NOTES

1.   For a more complete analysis of the aggregate demand and structural transformation theses, see Subcommittee on Economic Statistics, JEC, Higher Unemployment Rates, 1957-60: Structural Transformation or Inadequate Demand.

2.   A comparison of the social and individual costs of unemployment and inflation can be found in Economic Report of the President (1969), pp. 62-63.

3.   Paul M. Schwab, "Unemployment in the Ten Largest State and Major Regions," Employment and Earnings and Monthly Report on the Labor Force (May, 1969).

4.   Data provided by the West Virginia Department of Employment Security.

5.   Data provided by the Kentucky Department of Employment Security.

6.   "Measuring Unemployment and Subemployment in the Mississippi Delta," Monthly Labor Review, (April, 1969), p. 21.

7.   Data furnished by the Division of Research and Statistics, Department of Employment, State of California.

8.   See the Economic Report of the President (1969), p. 253 for data on changes in agricultural employment.

9.   Economic Report of the President (1969), p. 151.

10.   Ibid., p. 152.

11.   National Advisory Commission on Rural Poverty, The People Left Behind (Washington, D.C.: U.S. Government Printing Office, 1967), p. 3.

12.   Irwin Gray, "Employment Effect of a New Industry in a Rural Area," Monthly Labor Review (June, 1969), 26-30.

13.   Ibid., p. 29.

14.   U. S. Bureau of the Census, unpublished tabulations.

CHAPTER **7** RELOCATION PROGRAMS
IN THE UNITED STATES

INTRODUCTION

In Canada and the countries of western Europe, relocation
programs form part of overall manpower programs which are
designed to raise the productivity of workers. All governments that use labor mobility programs use them to move unemployed or underemployed workers out of areas with few
employment opportunities to areas in which labor is in short
supply. The basic objective of these programs is to transfer
given skills to places where they generate a higher marginal
physical product. Great Britain and a few other countries use
relocation allowances to channel highly skilled workers to
selected areas where their skills are in short supply. By
using labor mobility programs, governments are underwriting
some or all of the risks of workers who probably would not
move, in return for reasonable pay-offs through a more efficient allocation of the labor force. This rationale is sound,
for little is to be gained by subsidizing their unemployment
in the home area.

Canada and Sweden have the most liberal labor mobility
programs of all Western nations, and attach comparatively
greater importance to them. In Canada, any unemployed or
underemployed worker who has a permanent offer of employment in another community is eligible for relocation assistance. This assistance provides for travel and household
removal expenses, housing allowances, and resettlement
grants of up to $1,000. On a per capita basis, the Canadian
government allocates roughly ten times more for its labor
mobility program than does the United States. Sweden has
the most comprehensive labor mobility program of all countries. In 1968 approximately 22,000 Swedish workers received relocation allowances to secure employment. In
addition to the standard relocation allowances, compensation
is also provided for losses incurred in the sale of a house.

159

The United States is the only major industrial country without a national labor mobility program. Experimental projects exist through the provision of an authorization of $5 million under the Manpower Development and Training Act. These projects involve moving workers from a few extremely depressed areas and locating them in selected receiving areas where jobs or training facilities are available. There has been general opposition to a national program for relocating unemployed or underemployed workers. Politicians fear that an induced migration from areas that are already losing population will endanger their political careers. Business firms resent the loss of a cheap labor supply and a source of demand for their products. Then there is the sentiment that anyone who is worth his salt should bestir himself if he is unemployed and look elsewhere for employment. Undoubtedly, Americans are a mobile people, but the costs of mobility and the lack of knowledge of existing employment opportunities can be a deterrent to many people. There are other factors which impinge upon labor mobility--home ownership, attachment to the home area, and a lack of marketable job skills.

A national program of relocation assistance would appear to be an important adjunct of manpower policy. In order to improve the ability of the United States to maintain unemployment consistently below a level of 4 percent without placing substantial pressure on the level of prices, manpower policy can play an important role. Manpower programs can improve the productivity of the labor force, and hence increase total output and the rate of economic growth. Relocation assistance coupled with job training can move workers from areas with few employment opportunities into areas where jobs are available and where the marginal physical product per worker is higher.

In general, there are several groups of workers who would benefit by a program of relocation assistance. First of all, there are those workers who have been replaced as a result of changes in technology or a decline in industry in a particular area. The coal mining industry is a case in point. Reference has been made in several of the preceding chapters to a decline in coal mining employment in many of the industrial nations. The United States faces a similar situation, for in many coal mining areas employment has

declined by more than 50 percent over the last two decades.
Moreover, some of these areas are inaccessible to transportation and lack a resource base to attract alternative
industries. Secondly, other groups of workers, though not
necessarily unemployed, live in rural areas with few employment opportunities. Although the idea of encouraging industry
to locate in rural areas is commendable, and in many areas
plausible, there will still be areas which will remain without
industry. Finally, there are culturally and racially disadvantaged groups who need special training and assistance in
order to participate in the economic life of the nation. This
would include people from mountain and other socially isolated
areas.

Benefits of Relocation

The rationale for the use of relocation rests upon the
expectation of a series of benefits that should redound to the
advantage of those workers who are relocated, as well as to
those areas that receive them. These benefits can be cate-
gorized as primary and secondary benefits. (This analysis
is based upon the use of a cost-benefit model which was developed by the Planning and Evaluation Branch of the Department of Manpower and Immigration in Canada.)

Primary benefits would be the gains in both money and
real incomes to relocated workers which would more than
counterbalance losses in money and real income in the home
area. Since the typical worker who receives relocation
assistance is unemployed, these losses may be minimal.
There could also be gains in money and real incomes if other
members of a worker's family secured employment. Finally,
there would be an increase in total output attributable to those
workers who are relocated, and to other members of their
families who secure employment. From the standpoint of an
increase in output, the demand or receiving area would gain.

Perhaps the most important secondary benefit that could
result from relocation is the easing of pressures on prices
as more jobs are filled and labor shortages become less
acute. Then, too, the increase in employment will have a
multiplier effect which would provide an additional stimulus

to economic activity in the demand area. There are also
certain social benefits, such as a greater overall sense of
family security brought about by employment and job satisfaction, which also have to be considered.

Costs of Relocation

Balanced against the benefits of relocation are certain
costs which have to be measured. These costs can be psychological as well as financial. Investment theory rules out
psychic costs, on the grounds that workers take them into
account anyway in calculating their marginal rates of sub-
stitution of work for leisure. It follows that mobility incentives that are concerned with overcoming psychological costs
would upset the necessary optimizing condition. But there
is a distinction between ex ante and ex post satisfactions.
Families undoubtedly have a high psychological attachment
to familiar areas--but once they move and establish new
roots, their sentiments and preference functions change.

Primary costs would include the actual financial costs
of relocation, including the administrative costs, and the
loss of real output attributable to the workers in their old
jobs. However, the loss of real output would be negligible
if the workers were unemployed in the home area. Economists define costs of production of a particular product as
the value of the forgone alternative products that resources
used in its production could have produced. The costs of
resources are their values in their best alternative uses.
This is the opportunity cost doctrine. To an unemployed
worker, his opportunity cost is zero if there are no sources
of employment.

One secondary cost would be a negative multiplier effect
in the home area which is brought about by the outmigration
of workers and their families. This means a loss of purchasing power to business firms, a loss which may be minimal because the workers are unemployed. This point, however, does have validity and must be considered. Another
secondary cost is an increase in the demand for social overhead capital facilities in the areas in which workers are relocated. Social costs also have to be considered. For one

thing, there might be greater family uncertainty and insecurity caused by the transition from a familiar to an unfamiliar environment. Also, social tension could develop as a result of increased congestion and urban overcrowding.

The basic desideratum in a relocation program is an improvement in the earnings of the workers who are moved. It is to be emphasized that relocation is no substitute for occupational preparation, including basic education. It cannot be assumed that rural people, when relocated in an urban setting, will automatically improve their incomes. In fact, in some cases the reverse may well be true.[1] Successful relocation programs in Canada and Sweden are tied to job training and judicious placement policies on the part of the national employment services of the two countries. Relocation by itself can do little or nothing to overcome the disabilities incurred through the lack of individual preparation for employment.

DEVELOPMENT OF RELOCATION PROGRAMS

Relocation assistance was provided for in the 1963 amendments to the Manpower Development and Training Act. Section 208 authorized the Secretary of Labor to carry out, in a limited number of geographic areas, pilot projects designed to assess or demonstrate the effectiveness of relocation in reducing unemployment, and also to examine their operation and economic and social implications. The assistance was provided in the form of loans, grants, or both to unemployed individuals who could not be expected to find full-time employment in the home area, and who had bona fide offers of employment elsewhere and were qualified to perform the work. These basic criteria have been maintained in subsequent amendments to the Manpower Development and Training Act. (The Trade Expansion Act provided allowances for the relocation of workers who lost employment as a result of reductions in tariffs promoted by the act: Unemployed heads of families who have little prospect of finding suitable and gainful employment in their home communities and have been offered long-term employment elsewhere are eligible to receive relocation allowances which cover the moving expenses of the worker and his family and the cost of moving household goods.)

Hearings held by the House Committee on Education and Labor in 1963 had found considerable support in favor of relocation assistance.[2] It was recognized that many depressed areas lack the resource base to attract industry, and that a partial solution to the problem of unemployment and under-employment is to induce some workers to leave these areas. It was also recognized that many unemployed workers in de-pressed areas can be placed in other areas in which there is a shortage of labor. In a survey of 150,000 unemployed workers in Illinois, 31 percent indicated that they would be willing to move to other areas of employment.

The 1965 amendment to the Manpower Development and Training Act extended the mobility program to June 30, 1967,[3] and provided for more liberal use of grants--removing a 50-percent restriction provided earlier--and for more liberal loans, which were subject to the following conditions:[4]

1.   There was reasonable assurance of repayment of the loan;

2.   Credit was not available on reasonable terms from private sources or other federal, state, or local pro-grams;

3.   The amount of the loan, together with other funds, was adequate to achieve the purpose for which the loan was intended;

4.   The loan bore interest at a rate not less than the average market yield on outstanding Treasury obligations, plus additional charges, if any, toward covering the cost of the program; and

5.   The loan was repayable within not more than 10 years.

Up to $5 million a year was authorized for carrying out the relocation assistance programs. Initial and subsequent pilot projects which were sponsored under the Manpower Act were designed with the aim of trying to relocate a variety of groups of unemployed workers in various geographic settings in order to test a set of assumptions about relocation. Al-though these assumptions have been mentioned previously, they form the basic rationale for the use of relocation assistance, and should be repeated.

     1.   Labor demand in one area can be matched against an excess labor supply in another area;

     2.   The financial costs of moving can deter the mobility of many unemployed workers; and

     3.   The benefits to society and to the workers of providing relocation assistance can more than offset the monetary and real costs of relocation. Among the direct benefits would be an increase in real output and income to the workers moved, and among the direct costs would be an increase in the demand for social overhead capital facilities in the areas to which workers were sent.

Initial Labor Mobility Projects

Labor mobility projects were first conducted in 1965 by state employment security agencies in California, Illinois, Indiana, Kentucky, Minnesota, Missouri, Montana, New York, Utah, Virginia, and West Virginia, and by five private organizations: three universities, one nonprofit foundation, and one national social welfare nonprofit association. These organizations conducted projects based in Alabama, Illinois, Indiana, Michigan, and North Carolina. An indication of the variety and nature of these projects can be provided by an outline of their objectives.

One set of projects focused on a specific group of workers, such as all graduates of a Manpower Development and Training Act project, or workers involved in a mass lay-off. These projects were located in Indiana, Utah, and Virginia. The purpose of the Indiana project was to relocate graduates of an MDTA training course in South Bend, which at that time was a labor surplus area, in other parts of Indiana. However, an improvement in local economic conditions resulted in an upturn in employment opportunities and a reduction in the actual number of workers relocated. It was found that those who were relocated had serious employment problems attributable to a lack of basic education despite their skill training.

The Utah project was for workers laid off the preceding winter by the Thiokol Chemical Company's missile plant in Brigham City. This is a sparsely settled part of northern Utah where the employment, aside from the Thiokol plant, is essentially in agriculture. The 1964 unemployment rate for the area was 6.2 percent. In general, workers were re-located at other plants within the aerospace industry, and the relocation program was rated as successful from the stand-point of meeting emergencies such as mass lay-offs. However, the workers possessed skills that were transferable to other companies.

In Virginia, the relocatees were taken from four depressed coal mining counties--all with unemployment rates in excess of 10 percent--in the southwestern part of the state, and re-located in other areas of the state. Relocation was to such cities as Alexandria, Newport News, Norfolk, and Richmond, where labor was in short supply. The relocatees were se-lected from a project population which consisted of 500 MDTA graduates and an equal number of workers who had applied for MDTA training--many of whom were former coal miners. There was a high rate of return to the home area, which was attributable to several factors--a higher cost of living and a scarcity of housing in the cities, the attractiveness of welfare payments and lower living costs in the home area, and diffi-culty in adjusting to an urban environment.

The second set of projects dealt with a sample selection of unemployed workers in an area, generally taken from public employment service active files. These projects were located in California, Kentucky, Minnesota, and West Vir-ginia. In California, the supply area was metropolitan San Diego, which had had substantial unemployment rates for the previous four years. The project population was obtained by drawing every 16th applicant from the active file of the San Diego local office of the California State Employment Service. Very few persons were actually relocated, and there was a general reluctance to move which was attributable to ideal climate and living conditions in San Diego and to an upturn in employment.

In Kentucky, the relocatees were selected from Floyd, Johnson, Martin, and Magoffin counties, in the coal mining eastern part of the state. In 1964, the unemployment rates

for these counties ranged from 13.2 percent in Floyd County
to 29.7 percent in Magoffin County. (In 1968, the unemployment rates for the same counties were as follows: Floyd
County, 11.5 percent; Johnson County, 12.7 percent; Martin
County, 20 percent; and Magoffin County, 18.2 percent.)
The population from which the relocatees were selected was
the active file of unemployed in the Prestonburg office of the
Kentucky State Employment Service. Major job placement
areas were Louisville, Lexington, and other areas in Kentucky.
A small number of workers were relocated, and the rate of
return to the home area was high. The most important reason
for the high rate of return was the attractiveness of welfare
benefits in the home area, compared with wages in the outside
area.

    In Minnesota, the relocatees were selected from a 15-
county supply area in the northeastern part of the state. This
area had high and persistent unemployment as a result of a
declining demand for labor in the mining of iron ore. The
demand or receiving area was Minneapolis-St. Paul. A small
number of workers were actually relocated. The primary
reason was that the so-called "Taconite Amendment" brought
expectations of new prosperity in the supply area.

    In West Virginia, the supply area was Boone, Logan,
McDowell, and Wyoming counties, in the depressed coal
mining area in the southern part of the state. Unemployment
rates in 1964 ranged from 15.4 percent for Boone County to
7.3 percent in Wyoming County. The project population was
derived by taking a 20 percent sample of the active files in
the employment service files in Logan and Welch. Over 90
percent of West Virginia's relocations were outside the state,
as there was little potential for moving to jobs within the state.
The rate of return to the home area was around 50 percent,
but in general the relocation project could be rated as a success. It did indicate, however, that additional services were
needed than merely matching workers with jobs and providing
relocation assistance.

    In a third set of projects, the worker group was not se-
lected for inclusion prior to project operation. Instead, they
were recruited during the project on the basis of geographic
location and interest in participating in the relocation program.
In Illinois, a six-county area in the southern part of the state

was the supply area. These counties were similar to the areas involved in the Kentucky, West Virginia, and Virginia projects in that the primary industry was coal mining. In Missouri, the supply area was seven counties in the southeastern "bootheel" portion of the state. There is a high percentage of low-income, underemployed farm workers in the area. The relocation project focused on these farm workers. In Montana, the supply area was Carbon, Musselshell, and Stillwater counties, which are in different parts of the state. The unemployment rate in the three counties was 7.5 percent in 1964. Relocation was within the state and in contiguous states.

New York presented an arrangement different from those of the other labor mobility projects--one which may well have significant implications for the future. The supply area was Nassau and Suffolk counties on Long Island. The economy of these counties depends to a major degree on defense spending. In 1965, many workers, including skilled engineers and technicians, were laid off by Republic Aviation as a result of the completion of several defense contracts. Local jobs to match the skills of these workers were not available, and engineers had to take jobs in filling stations or selling insurance. Lack of funds to move elsewhere was one factor in tying these persons to the area. However, large numbers of those laid off had skills in demand elsewhere, and relocation was in general successful.

In addition to the 11 projects carried out by state employment security offices, five other projects were carried out by private organizations. One, administered by the North Carolina Fund, sought to relocate hardcore unemployed persons from rural coastal plains counties to small industrial counties in the Piedmont areas of the state. Another, conducted by Tuskegee Institute, focused on graduates of a prison training program as well as other workers recruited generally from rural Alabama areas. Virtually all were Negroes. A third, conducted by Northern Michigan University, was designed to move MDTA training course enrollees from the Northern Peninsula to downstate Michigan and Wisconsin jobs.

Eligibility Requirements For Relocation

Conditions for eligibility were the same for all of the pilot projects:

1.   The worker had to be involuntarily unemployed. (An involuntarily unemployed individual is unemployed through no fault of his own; or unemployed for six or more weeks regardless of cause; or a member of a farm family with less than $1, 200 annual net farm income.)

2.   The worker could not be expected to secure full-time employment within commuting distance of his regular place of residence.

3.   The worker had to obtain suitable employment or a bona fide offer of employment that could reasonably be expected to be of long-term duration, in the area in which he desired to relocate.

4.   The worker had to be selected for relocation and had to file an application for relocation assistance with the agency conducting the project.

Coverage of Relocation Allowances

Relocation allowances were made available (with some variations) in the initial projects for the following expense items:

1.   A travel allowance to defray the cost of moving a worker and his family from the home area to the area of relocation. This allowance was to cover the most economical form of public transportation from the home area to the new area or, if the worker's own automobile was used, 10 cents a mile was to be provided for the usually traveled route between the home area and the new area, with no additional allowance for family members traveling in the same automobile.

2.   A household goods moving allowance for the transportation of household goods from the home area to the

new location. The worker had to provide at least two estimates
from moving firms regularly engaged in the shipping of household goods, with the allowance to be equal to the lower of the
two estimates. (The allowance was not to exceed the cost of
moving 7,000 pounds net weight for a worker and his family,
or 2,500 pounds net weight if the worker was single.) If the
worker used a trailer to transport his household goods, he
was allowed 12 cents a mile to cover his automobile and trailer.

        3.   A temporary storage allowance to cover the actual
expenses of storage of household goods for a period of up to
30 days.

        4.   A lump-sum allowance to defray the cost of living
expenses for the worker and his family while traveling to the
new location, and for incidental expenses pending the receipt
of the first paycheck. The amount of the basic allowance was
set at the national average weekly manufacturing wage, with
an additional 50 percent of that sum for each member of the
family, up to a minimum of three times the basic allowance.

Method of Payment

The relocation allowance (travel, removal of furniture,
storage, and lump-sum) ranged from 50 to 100 percent of the
cost. The amount paid depended on whether the particular
project provided for a grant, loan, or combination of both.
Most projects provided for a 50 percent grant plus a 50 percent loan; several provided only loans. The loans were made
available on an interest-free basis, with repayment spread
over a three-year basis.

The financial assistance actually provided varied greatly
by project, by distance of move, by size of family, and by
amount of household goods. The average assistance was
around $300.

The initial labor mobility projects were varied in nature.
Their aim was to try to relocate a variety of groups of unemployed workers in various geographic settings. Since these
pilot projects were limited and experimental in nature, no
comparison can be made between them and the well-established

Canadian and European relocation programs. The objectives, procedures, and settings of the projects varied considerably-- from focus, as in North Carolina, on moving low-income rural farm workers to cities, to efforts in West Virginia to move unemployed coal miners to jobs in other states, to concentration, in New York, on the movement of laid-off engineers and skilled technicians.

Some general conclusions can be reached concerning the results of the projects. Relocation assistance coupled with effective job placement did influence a number of workers to leave their home areas. The cost of travel and the removal of furniture and other household effects can be a significant deterrent to mobility, particularly since a substantial number of unemployed workers possess no liquid assets. Although Americans are a mobile people in general, their mobility is enhanced by the possession of savings or the ability to secure a loan to finance the move. Most unemployed or low-income workers do not qualify on either count.

The rate of return to the home area was quite high for several projects. The most important reasons for the return were the inability to find adequate housing and higher living costs in the demand area. A number of workers also had problems in adjusting to a new environment, illustrating the fact that supportive or counseling services are needed in addition to relocation allowances and job placement. The turnover rate at the new place of employment was high for relocatees. However, this turnover was not excessive when compared with the normal turnover rates for many plants at which the relocatees were employed. Most of the workers who received relocation assistance were employed in low-paying jobs, but the comparison with the alternative of no or partial employment in the home area was quite favorable even when certain social overhead costs were taken into consideration.

EXTENSION OF LABOR MOBILITY PROJECTS

The first set of labor mobility demonstration projects was extended into the periods 1966-67 and 1967-68, and was expanded to include a greater number of potential relocatees.

In North Carolina, for example, the supply area was expanded from six to 42 counties. Kentucky expanded its project to include the relocation of unemployed family heads completing the Work Experience and Training Program in 19 depressed coal mining counties. Some modifications were made in the amount of relocation allowances, and more effort was made to provide supportive services for the relocatees. The Travelers Aid Agency was used in some projects to provide post-relocation counseling, assistance in obtaining housing in the demand area, and basic orientation and adaptation in the new area. For those projects where no Travelers Aid or other supportive agencies were available, responsibility for providing these services was assumed by the relocating agency.

New projects were added, and relocation objectives continued to vary. In California, relocation was provided to skilled workers who were laid off by an aircraft company. Although it might appear illogical to relocate skilled workers who presumably have the resources to move themselves, the point can be made that in some cases workers who are laid off accept jobs with lower skill requirements or remain unemployed. The gain to society in terms of an increase in total output can be considerable if these workers can be induced to relocate in areas in which their skill can be fully utilized. A similar relocation project was undertaken in Pennsylvania, where a lay-off in a glass factory occurred. Jobs were available at other glass plants under the provisions of an industry-wide union contract, but no provision was made for relocation assistance. To encourage mobility, relocation allowances were provided by the state employment office to those who wished to move. The majority of workers who were laid off found employment, usually at lower wages, and remained in the home area.

In Texas, relocation assistance was provided to Mexican-American workers in the Rio Grande Valley who had received MDTA training. The primary place of relocation was the Ling-Temco-Vaught plant near Dallas. On-the-job training was provided by the employer. Approximately 1,000 workers were relocated from the Rio Grande area, and the success rate, measured in terms of retention of workers at the place of employment, was high.

In Washington, a reverse type of labor mobility project was developed. Instead of dealing with the outmigration of

workers from labor surplus areas, this project was designed
to facilitate inmigration to a geographical area experiencing
a high level of industrial expansion. This area included the
cities of Seattle and Everett. Since unemployed workers
possessing the required skills could not be found within this
area, unemployed qualified workers were sought in other
areas of Washington and in seven neighboring states. Evidence from this labor mobility project indicates that the relocation of workers can be used as a means of reducing unemployment by balancing labor surplus and labor shortage
areas.

In Iowa and Mississippi, projects were designed to relocate displaced agricultural workers. In Iowa, the purpose
of the project was to provide various manpower services,
including information about existing job opportunities, to
rural unemployed and low-income workers in the southern
part of the state. Relocation assistance was provided to some
workers, but the majority of moves required no such assistance. In Mississippi, the relocation project was designed
to help move unemployed Negro sharecropper or day laborers
who were no longer needed on cotton farms in the Delta region.
Relocation areas included Memphis, Tennessee, and Jackson,
Tupelo, Hattiesburg, and Pascagoula within the state. All of
these demand areas were industrialized, with solid growth
potential and firm employment levels. Basic education and
some form of vocational training were provided to the relocatees,
and emphasis was placed upon counseling as a component of
total relocation assistance.

Probably the most ambitious relocation effort was one
which involved the United States Employment Service and 18
affiliated state employment service agencies. Relocation
projects in 12 states were linked together in order to ascertain
how the employment service could operate a national relocation
program. Twelve state projects were operated within the
framework of a common set of standards, including payment
procedures and eligibility criteria. An interregional job
clearance system was provided to place persons who wished
to relocate.

RESULTS OF RELOCATION PROJECTS

It is necessary to remember that the relocation projects which were undertaken during the period 1965-68 were experimental in nature and diverse in their objectives. Some projects worked with disadvantaged persons from rural areas, while other projects handled workers who were involved in permanent lay-offs. One project relocated parolees from a state prison. In some cases, workers who had received job training under the provisions of the Manpower Development and Training Act were relocated; in other cases, workers who had no job skills were relocated. Projects were administered by state and local employment security offices, and by private organizations. Methods of recruitment and placement also varied. For some projects, hiring interviews were conducted locally by out-of-state employers, but generally, recruitment efforts for relocatees depended on the regular flow of applicants to the local employment service offices. Some projects employed recruiters whose purpose was to find persons who were willing to relocate.

Altogether, there were 37 relocation projects in 28 states and 12, 234 workers were relocated with relocation assistance. [5] An additional 1, 494 workers were relocated without relocation assistance, bringing the total number of persons relocated to 13, 728. The cost of relocation, including administrative costs, amounted to $9 million over the period the projects were in effect. Comparisons can be made with the Canadian and Swedish relocation programs. In Canada, for the fiscal years 1967-68 and 1968-69 12, 791 workers were relocated at a cost of $5. 9 million. The Canadian program, however, is operated on a national basis by the Department of Manpower and Immigration. In Sweden, $6 million was spent on relocation in the fiscal year 1967-68, and some 22, 500 workers were relocated. Relocation is a national program operated by the Royal Labor Market Board. It is to be admitted, however, that different institutional factors in Sweden make a national relocation program relatively easy to administer and operate--factors which include the existence of a homogeneous and highly literate population. But, contrary to what some people seem to believe, the Swedish government does not exercise autocratic control over the labor market and the economy.

It would be expected that relocation programs could reduce the economic and social waste of unemployment and underemployment. Of course, there are other ways in which this
can be done. For example, the federal government could provide a job to every unemployed person who is willing and able
to work. Another alternative is a national program of tax
incentives, grants, or loans to induce industry to locate in
areas where unemployment is prevalent. However, there is
no convincing evidence to indicate that this type of approach
would be more than moderately successful. It has been estimated that in North Carolina alone there will be a deficit of
some 120,000 jobs in the rural coastal counties by 1970. It
is to be seriously doubted that tax incentives would attract
even a small fraction of the industry necessary to provide
employment for everyone in this area. Even though the use
of tax incentives has merit on value grounds, it is more difficult to justify this approach on the basis of efficiency.

In an evaluation of the results of the relocation projects,
one gain appears to be evident. Relocation as a part of a
national manpower policy can have a favorable effect on the
rather aimless direction of rural-to-urban migration. In its
report, The People Left Behind, the President's National
Advisory Commission on Rural Poverty refers to a deficiency
in the natural mobility process which has caused millions of
people to exchange life in a rural slum for life in an urban
slum. Most of these persons had no training, nor any prospective job, when they arrived in the cities.[6] Often, many
months were spent in finding employment. Relocation assistance could bring an improvement in labor market adjustments
on the part of workers moving from rural to urban areas by
providing job offers before the move, and moving expenses
to the place of employment. Greater economic rationality
can then be provided to migration. It is to be reiterated, however, that relocation assistance would only be one part of a
national manpower program, which would also include job
training and the improvement of basic educational skills.

The relocation assistance projects concentrated primarily
on moving unemployed workers. The majority of persons relocated were employed for a period of 14 weeks or less, and
generally were either experienced industrial workers who had
been laid off through plant closures or cutbacks, and unskilled
workers who were either seasonally or intermittently unemployed,

or who were out of the labor market. One of the lessons
learned from the projects was that workers have a better
chance for a successful relocation if they are moved before
they become long-term unemployed and lose whatever work
skills they had.[7] A reduction in the duration of unemployment can be considered a positive benefit of the relocation
projects.

The level of education of the relocatees varied from
project to project. One study involving 1,529 relocatees
reported that 40 percent were high school graduates and 10
percent had some college training. However, 25 percent of
the relocatees had only a grammar school education or less.
In some cases, the worker's educational background was
improved by MDTA training.

In measuring the effectiveness of any relocation program,
it is necessary to consider the extent to which workers remain at their jobs once they have been relocated. It would
appear logical to include as successful relocations those
workers who remain employed at their original jobs, or at
other jobs after relocation. If workers move to other jobs
in the relocation area, or even to jobs in other areas, relocation should be considered a success. So perhaps the
obtaining and retention of employment, regardless of where
it finally is, can be considered one of the basic success criteria for a relocation program.

In the relocation projects, a worker was considered to
be successfully relocated if he remained in the demand area
two months after relocation. This is a rather generous success criterion. Actually, the rate of return to the home area
was rather high for many projects when a longer time period
was taken into consideration. Mobility projects operated in
North Carolina reported that only 33 percent of those persons
relocated remained in the demand area during the first contract
period, and 39 percent remained during the second contract
period. Although the majority of those who left the demand
area returned to the home area, a number of workers moved
to other areas within or outside of the state, and some workers
entered the military service. Perhaps a positive factor is
that for some persons the home ties or fear of the cities was
broken to the extent that they were willing to move to jobs
outside of the demand area. In some cases, those relocatees

who returned home improved their economic position over
what it was before they left; in other cases the reverse was
true.

Single persons under the age of 25 are the most likely to
be unsuccessful relocatees. In several projects, as many as
50 percent of those who returned to the home area were single.
It appears that the young worker is not ready to settle down
permanently, but is in a state of restlessness. He is not
mature enough to realize that he must accept responsibility
for himself, and he is not sure of his goal in life. This im-
maturity and negative attitude on the part of the young unsuccessful relocatee is often the result of the economically de-
prived environment of the area from which he came. Usually
he is poorly educated and has worked intermittently at unskilled
or low-skilled jobs. The inclusion of single youths would present a problem for a successful national relocation program.

Housing has proved to be the most important physical
block to an efficient operation of the labor mobility projects.
(In the state of Washington, labor mobility project, 264 relocatees listed housing as the main disadvantage of relocation,
compared with 34 relocatees who listed crowded conditions of
city living as the main disadvantage.) Housing is scarce in
many areas for low-income families, and federal projects
have long waiting lists. (The Virginia relocation project, faced
with a shortage of housing, developed an agreement with a
large mobile home sales organization to establish trailer parks
and provide mobile homes to relocatees upon payment of $300;
this sum was advanced to the relocatees as a loan, and the
total monthly payments for all housing expenses were less
than $100, which was below comparable housing rentals.)
Private housing at a rent level unskilled industrial workers
can pay, when it can be found, is often substandard. The lack
of such housing is a result of the economics of supply and
demand. Land is a scarce resource in most industrial areas
and its cost is high. Therefore, the rent must be high in order
to give the owners a return on their investment. Thus, available housing is usually in the form of high-rent apartment
buildings or expensive homes which the relocatees can't afford.
Good low-rent housing does not exist because it would be uneconomical; owners would not get a sufficient return on their
investment. The alternative available housing is often the
slum--which, of course, is undesirable.

On an a priori basis, one of the strongest arguments
that can be made for a national program of relocation assistance is that the monetary and real gains to the individual and
to society should more than counterbalance the cost of moving
workers and the loss in terms of monetary and real incomes
that the workers experience in leaving the home area. It is
apparent from reviewing the results of some of the relocation
projects that enormous monetary gains can result from the
relocation of workers. However, there is the necessary
proviso that the workers remain in the demand area for at
least six months or probably longer.

It may well be true that the cost of relocation, in comparison with other employment alternatives, is lower relative
to the possible benefits that can be derived. Before-and-after-
relocation earnings have been provided for five 1967-68 labor
mobility projects which were responsible for moving around
3,000 relocatees.[8] The average wage earned on the last
regular job prior to relocation was $1.80 an hour. However,
more than 90 percent of the relocatees were unemployed prior
to relocation, and their average length of unemployment was
21.3 weeks. Forty percent of the relocatees were either
receiving unemployment compensation or welfare assistance
at the time of relocation.

The average starting wage on the new job was $2.25 an
hour. For the 3,000 workers who were relocated, the total
weekly income amounted to approximately $270,000. Although
the cost for relocation allowances varied from project to
project, the average cost of relocation was $325 per relocatee,
and the approximate cost of moving 3,000 relocatees was
$1,000.000. In four weeks, assuming that all of the relocatees
remained employed, the total monetary gain would have been
$1,080,000. If 60 percent of the relocatees were still em-
ployed at the average starting wage after two months, their
gain in earnings would have been around $1,400,000.

However, differentials in real income may be narrowed
considerably. Many relocatees, particularly from the rural
areas, had the benefit of free rent and home-produced foods
while living in the home area. One study of relocatees who
moved from rural North Carolina counties to cities within the
state indicated that savings in food, rent, fuel, and transportation counterbalanced a higher monetary income in the

cities for some relocatees.[9] Many relocatees had no rental
costs in the home area, but averaged paying $70.00 in the
cities. Food costs were in general half of what they were in
the cities. So an income differential of $2,000 a year between
the rural areas and the cities can be narrowed to the extent
that the real income differential is much smaller than the
apparent money income differential; and the cost of not relocating, or returning home after relocation, carries a smaller
penalty than otherwise would be the case. It is also likely
that many relocatees would consider only short-run differences
in income, and would make comparisons between rural and
urban living using this perspective.

This comparison also tends to discount the benefits that
can redound to the advantage of the relocatees. This would
include better police protection, street lights, sewers, treated
water, medical care, and fire protection. There would be
better schools with more facilities, so that education would
be far superior to that provided in the rural areas. In fact,
poverty and lack of opportunity can be correlated with poor
education. In short, the level of living can be much higher
in the urban areas than it is in the rural areas. Most of the
potential gains cannot be valued adequately or accurately;
however, it is important to know that although basic real-
income differences between rural and urban areas can be
narrow, relocatees can enjoy a potential gain in moving that,
although difficult to quantify, can be considerable.

Evaluations of relocation projects have generally shown
favorable results. Dr. Gerald Somers of the University of
Wisconsin took a group of relocatees in projects in Michigan
and Wisconsin and a control group possessing similar characteristics which did not relocate.[10] Both groups had been employed in agriculture, mining, construction, and trade in the
home area. Those who were relocated secured employment
primarily in industrial plants. Somers found that those who
were relocated and remained in the demand area suffered far
less from unemployment than those who did not relocate and
those who relocated but later returned home--some 20 percent
of the relocatees. Moreover, a favorable occupational shift
toward professional and technical occupations, and out of
semi-skilled and unskilled categories, was much more marked
among relocatees who remained in the demand area. Also,
although there was little difference between the average weekly

earnings of movers, nonmovers, and returnees in the year
prior to relocation, a significant difference between the movers
and the other two groups occurred in the period following relocation. A high percentage of MDTA training graduates were
among those who moved and those who did not; and the improvement in income and employment experienced by the movers
was considerable.

A merit of relocation assitance is that it can provide
some upward mobility in terms of occupational skills. Table
23 presents a distribution of occupations before and after relocation for five relocation projects which were responsible
for the moves of 50 percent of the total number of relocatees
during the period 1967-68.

The results of the relocation projects tend to confirm
orthodox economic theory. Workers respond to expected
earnings differentials, and distance adds a barrier to mobility
both by raising the cost of moving and by reducing the labor
market information available to workers. Personal characteristics, such as age, education, and race are significant
with respect to workers' initial motivations to move and their
ability to respond to opportunities. Single persons are more
willing to relocate than married persons, yet their rate of
return to the home area is much higher than the rate for married persons. Older persons, i.e. those 45 and over, and
the hardcore unemployed are the most difficult to relocate.
A low level of educational attainment also tends to mitigate
against successful relocation. Extensive supportive services
appear to be a necessary desideratum for the unskilled, the
long-term unemployed, and the rural worker with little or no
history of employment.

Advantages of a National Relocation Program

Relocation assistance cannot be considered as a basic
panacea for labor surplus areas. It does, however, possess
several advantages which make it worthy of inclusion as a
part of a comprehensive national manpower program. These
advantages center around an improvement in the functioning
of the labor market.

TABLE 23

Occupational Distribution of Relocatees Before and After Relocation

	Percent
Occupational Distribution Before Relocation	
Professional and managerial	2.7
Clerical and sales	6.8
Service	10.5
Agriculture, forestry, and fisheries	3.7
Industrial and crafts	26.0
Unskilled and new entries into the labor market	50.3
	100.0
Occupational Distribution After Relocation	
Professional and managerial	2.5
Clerical and sales	5.3
Service	5.2
Agriculture, forestry, and fisheries	1.3
Industrial and crafts	49.9
Unskilled and new entries into the labor market	35.8
	100.0

Source: "Moving to Work," unpublished report prepared by the Labor Mobility Services Unit, Bureau of Employment Security, U.S. Employment Service.

1.   Relocation assistance helps to remove certain
obstacles to labor mobility. These include a lack of knowledge
of available job opportunities and a lack of financial resources
to facilitate movement to areas where jobs are available. Although a computerized job bank presumably can eliminate one
of these obstacles, at least to a major degree, the other ob-
stacle--a lack of money with which to move--still remains.
So relocation assistance, coupled with more effective job information and placement, can help match jobs with persons
who are stranded in chronically depressed labor surplus areas.

2.   Although there is a certain amount of overlap in
advantages, it would appear that a second advantage of relocation assistance is that it can be used to provide some sense of
direction and purpose in the migration of the types of persons
who, heretofore, have drifted rather aimlessly from one area
to another in search of employment. Often this aimless migration has piled thousands of untrained persons in the slums of
the major cities, where little possibility of employment exists
and unemployment rates are often well above the national rate.
In the experimental labor mobility demonstration projects which
have been recently completed by the Department of Labor,
more than half of the relocations in the fiscal year 1968 were
to cities with a population of less than 250,000 persons. [11]
Less than a tenth of all relocations were to large cities, although some of the smaller industrial receiving areas were
near metropolitan population centers. Conversely, however,
relocation does not appear to be particularly useful in re-
directing the flow of workers from urban ghettos to industrial
suburban areas or to less congested areas in general. It
appears that the return pull of the city, lack of interest in
moving, and racial discrimination mitigate against the successful relocation of workers from big city slum areas.

3.   In addition to providing greater economic rationality in migration, relocation can shift workers from intermittent employment or unemployment into jobs that provide
moderate wages. If relocation is linked with job training, the
effect on a favorable job retention rate is pronounced.

The population which a national relocation program would
serve would consist of two groups--disadvantaged workers
from areas where there is little likelihood of obtaining stable
employment, and unemployed workers who have been laid off

as a result of plant closures or other factors. The former
group is usually located in rural areas. Employment may be
seasonal or intermittent. Job skills are quite low, and the
education received by most is generally of an inferior quality.
The latter group may consist of coal miners or copper miners,
and other types of workers with job experience. To prevent
a deterioration in the job skills of these workers, relocation
is desirable in terms of the overall benefits to society. In this
respect, relocation assistance can be looked upon as a pre-
ventive measure in that skills have been preserved, not lost.

Relocation assistance would perhaps be more difficult to
administer when applied to unskilled workers from rural or
depressed areas. The poor socio-economic background in
these areas gives many workers less initiative or sophisti-
cation than workers in general, and they find it difficult to
adjust to conditions to which they are not accustomed. It is
apparent from reviewing some labor mobility projects that
were concerned with moving the rural poor, supportive services was the most important element in a successful relocation. Finding a person a job and providing him with the necessary travel assistance is not enough. In some cases, persons
who were relocated did not know how to mail a letter, dial a
phone, or shop in a supermarket. Supportive services, however, are not part of the functions performed by the United
States Employment Service, so it would appear logical that
responsibility for relocating the disadvantaged worker would
cut across agency lines.

On the other hand, experienced industrial workers who
have lost their jobs could be relocated through normal employment service channels. In this manner, a relocation program
would be similar to the national programs operated by the
employment services in the European countries. Some additional employment service personnel might be needed, but the
overall administrative problems involved in relocating unemployed industrial workers would be less than those involved
in relocating the rural poor.

Drawbacks to Relocation

In 1966 the Bureau of Employment Security recommended the creation of a permanent program of subsidized relocation, keyed to long-term unemployment, which would move 185, 000 workers a year. Even this relatively large number of relocations would be a small part of the total flow of worker migration that occurs annually between labor markets. It is estimated that 5 million persons in the labor force move between labor markets each year. It would appear that there are possibilities of perverting the objectives of a relocation program in that the federal government would pay for some moves that employers had formerly paid for. Although guidelines are easy to write, they are often difficult to enforce.

Of paramount importance to the success of any relocation program is the maintenance of a high level of aggregate demand, not only nationally but locally, in the areas in which workers are relocated. A reason for the effectiveness of relocation in Sweden is that labor shortages occasioned by a high level of economic activity continue to exist in the major industrial areas of the country. When there is a decline in aggregate demand, workers will be laid off and areas of labor surpluses will develop. Then a relocation program would be rather pointless. It is to be assumed that after the end of the Vietnam War, the federal government will have the necessary monetary and fiscal expertise to maintain national unemployment rates at a level of less than 4 percent.

Housing, or the lack of it, has been the major physical block to successful relocation. This holds true not only for the labor mobility demonstration projects in the United States, but for the national relocation programs of Canada and the European countries as well. Housing is scarce everywhere for low-income families. Federal housing projects have long waiting lists; low-rent housing is often below desirable minimum standards. If Negroes are involved in relocation, they are often quite difficult to place, as low-rent housing in some areas is segregated. With housing construction down in recent years, many areas face an acute housing shortage.

SUMMARY

Under the 1963 amendments to the Manpower Development and Training Act, authorization was provided for a series
of experimental labor mobility demonstration projects. These
projects had two important objectives--to test the effectiveness of relocation assistance in reducing the level of unemployment and to examine the operational, economic, and social
implications of such a program. In general, two categories
of workers were relocated by these projects--experienced,
and often skilled, workers who lost their jobs through plant
closures or through technological change; and unskilled and
often disadvantaged workers who were from rural or depressed areas, and who were unemployed or marginally employed in agriculture.

A total of 37 projects were funded in 28 states during a
period from March 1965 to the end of 1968. State employment
services were responsible for the operation of some projects;
private contractors were responsible for others. During the
period of operations, 12,234 workers received relocation
assistance, and the total cost of relocation was around $9
million. The average cost per relocation was around $700.
Administrative costs per relocatee generally exceeded the
actual direct financial assistance. The primary reason for
high administrative costs was the need to provide counseling
and various supportive services. Direct financial assistance
varied by project, but in 1968 averaged $380 per relocatee.
Nearly half of the moves required allowances of $200 or less,
and only 10 percent required $800 or more. The amount of
the allowance also varied by workers--skilled workers moved
longer distances and required more financial assistance, unskilled workers moved shorter distances and required less.
However, unskilled workers required more extensive supportive services. This indicates that differing services are needed
for the successful relocation of unskilled rural workers and
for semi-skilled and skilled industrial workers.

The degree of success, measured in terms of the rate of
retention of the relocatees in the demand area, increased as
more experience was gained in the operation of relocation
projects. Follow-ups were limited to two months, and in
some cases four months, after relocation. Within this period,

an average of 20 percent of the relocatees had returned home,
and another 20 percent had changed jobs. It is quite likely,
however, that for most projects, around 30 percent of the
relocatees were actually at their original job in the demand
area a year after relocation. It should be pointed out that for
some industries, relocatee turnover was no different from
the normal turnover rate. Also, unlike the Canadian and
Swedish relocation programs, no exploratory grants were
given to relocatees for job interviews and for looking over the
company before making a decision. It is likely that the retention rate would be improved by providing exploratory grants
to potential relocatees.

There are those who would argue that it is more appropriate to allow the free forces of the labor market to bring
about the desired levels of labor mobility. However, in moves
that are unaided, kinship and ethnic patterns are often more
influential on location than the existence of economic opportunities. Migrants tend to move where others like them have
already settled. The end result is often a concentration of
unskilled workers in an area in which an oversupply already
exists. Relocation assistance provides some sort of economic
rationality in migration, in that workers are not sent into areas
where jobs are unavailable. Also, the free forces of the market don't provide the financial assistance to move workers
who have no savings and no knowledge of job opportunities in
other areas. A number of relocation projects indicated that
at least 90 percent of the workers relocated had no savings
whatsoever. It is suggested, then, that relocation assistance
can be used to fill the gap between the impoverished hardcore
unemployed and those who are motivated by the free forces of
the labor market. A goal of manpower policy should be to
reduce unemployment through training and planned relocation
to areas of high labor demand.

In general, the results of the experimental relocation
projects are favorable. The few cost-benefit studies that
have been done for individual projects report modest to favorable results. Improvements in post-relocation wages are
apparent. In addition to financial assistance in moving, guidance in surmounting the intricacies of moving and resettling
also proved to be important.

NOTES

1. Dale E. Hathaway and Brian E. Perkins, "Occupational Mobility and Migration from Agriculture, " Rural Poverty in the United States, A Report of the President's National Advisory Commission on Rural Poverty (1968), p. 185.

2. Manpower Development and Training Act hearings before the Select Committee on Labor of the Committee on Education and Labor, House of Representatives, 88th Congress, 1st sess., pp. 563, 610, 615, and 673.

3. See Report No. 170, "Manpower Act of 1965, " (to accompany H.R. 45227), 89th Congress, 1st sess., Sec. 104, p. 32.

4. See the Manpower Development and Training Act of 1962, as amended through October 24, 1968, Sec. 104.

5. Progress Report No. 2, Labor Mobility Study, prepared for the Office of Special Manpower Programs, Manpower Administration, by E.F. Shelley & Co., Inc. (June 20, 1969), p. 6.

6. President's National Advisory Commission on Rural Poverty, The People Left Behind (Washington, D.C.: U.S. Government Printing Office, 1967), p. ix.

7. Audrey Freedman, "Labor Mobility Projects for the Unemployed, " Monthly Labor Review, Bureau of Labor Statistics, xci (June 1968), 56-62.

8. "Moving to Work, " an unpublished report prepared by the Labor Mobility Services Unit, Bureau of Employment Security, U.S. Employment Service.

9. R.D. Robbins, "A Comparison of Real Incomes for Relocatees to Piedmont North Carolina from Rural Eastern North Carolina, " unpublished report for the North Carolina Fund.

10. Unpublished report prepared for the Department of Labor.

11. Freedman, op. cit., p. 60.

CHAPTER **8** A NATIONAL RELOCATION PROGRAM FOR THE UNITED STATES

INTRODUCTION

Relocation assistance is a useful manpower device. Although European experience has provided evidence of its usefulness, it has been tried only on an experimental basis in the United States, primarily because it was politically unpopular. During the first Senate hearings on the Area Redevelopment Act, a number of witnesses urged that the depressed areas program make provisions for relocating the unemployed in communities where there is a need for their skills. Relocation provisions were not only favored by academic representatives and spokesmen for labor groups, but also by representatives of business. Charles Taft, testifying for the National Trade Policy Commission, though expressing preference for a program which would bring jobs to depressed areas, urged also that the program be combined with relocation assistance where it was economically unfeasible to bring jobs to a depressed area.

However, there was bipartisan opposition to relocation assistance. In general, the arguments against relocation assistance were emotional, political, or economic. Senator Everett M. Dirksen, Republican from Illinois, invoked hearth and fireside against the subsidization of mobility, and drew an analogy between the American Indians who were willing to fight rather than to leave the graves of their ancestors, and later Americans who are willing to earn less or remain unemployed rather than leave home. [1] Senator Paul Douglas, Democrat from Illinois, argued on a more rational basis. He contended that a loss of social capital would be the end result if workers were encouraged to relocate. Investments in schools and community facilities would be wasted. Other politicians claimed

that relocation was cruel, inhuman, and unpatriotic--claims
prompted by the fact that it is much more desirable from a
political standpoint to be able to tell the voters that industry
is coming into one's district or state. But Congressional
views on relocation assistance apparently have undergone a
considerable transformation in recent years, as evidenced
by two bills recently introduced in Congress.

One bill, the "Manpower Act of 1969" (H. R. 11620), was
introduced by Congressman James O'Hara, Democrat from
Michigan and provides a rather comprehensive assortment
of manpower tools. It includes a program to provide incentives
to private and public employers to train or employ unemployed
or low-income workers. Special development efforts would
be made to provide job opportunities suited to the abilities of
the disadvantaged poor. Relocation assistance and other
special services would be provided to assist unemployed individuals and their families to relocate from a labor surplus
area to another area with expanding employment opportunities
where suitable jobs have been located. Preference for such
assistance would be given to persons who have received job
training before relocation, or who have been accepted for on-
the-job and other types of employer-directed training. Supportive services, including health services and counseling,
would be provided. Transportation costs would be paid in
order to encourage workers to attend skill training centers.

The second bill, "The Comprehensive Manpower Act of
1969" (H. R. 10908), was introduced by Congressman William
Steiger, Republican from Wisconsin, and would provide grants
to states on the condition that they submit comprehensive manpower plans to the Secretary of Labor. These plans would
provide for manpower training programs, which are supposed
to include any or all of a variety of services. For example,
a state plan could contain programs to provide part-time employment for students who are from low-income families.
Special programs could involve work activities directed to the
needs of the chronically unemployed or underemployed poor
who have poor employment prospects and are unable to secure
appropriate employment. Special training programs and skill
centers could also be established. Relocation assistance would
be given to unemployed persons to help relocate them and their
families in locations affording employment opportunities.

The Council of Economic Advisers, in the Economic
Report of the President for 1969, mentions relocation assistance as one measure which can be used to improve the labor
market in order to make higher levels of employment consistent with price stability. [2]   Labor market efficiency involves
the matching of job opportunities and available manpower.   To
improve labor mobility, it is necessary to provide workers
with improved information about job opportunities and training
programs which provide them with skills that are in short
supply.   The cost of moving can make it difficult for low-
income or unemployed workers to respond to employment
opportunities, so relocation assistance helps to break down
cost barriers to mobility.   The Council also refers to the use
of relocation assistance as a device for alleviating rural
poverty. [3]   While supporting programs that would diversify
the rural economy, the Council states that some rural communities, suited only for traditional resource-based industries,
will continue to decline.   Income maintenance, support for
education, job training and job location, and payment of the
costs of moving workers to jobs elsewhere are recommended.

A NATIONAL PROGRAM OF
RELOCATION ASSISTANCE

Relocation assistance was included among the many
policy recommendations made by President Nixon's public
welfare and manpower task forces, and was incorporated into
his overall manpower development program which was recently
submitted to Congress (H.R. 13742, "The Manpower Training
Act of 1969").   The purpose of this program is to involve all
levels of government in the creation of a national manpower
plan.   To emphasize a decentralization of manpower activities,
the program provides grants to states for a variety of purposes,
including the provision of institutional and on-the-job occupational training for employed and unemployed workers, and the
provision of relocation assistance, including grants, loans,
and the furnishing of additional services which would aid an
involuntarily unemployed individual to relocate in an area
where he could obtain suitable employment.

A national computerized job bank program is one part
of the Nixon manpower policy. This program is supposed to
provide a means of matching the qualifications of unemployed,
underemployed, and disadvantaged workers with employer
requirements on a national, state, or local basis. The approach has merit in that it can more expeditiously match job
skills to job requirements, and reduce the amount of time
spent in unemployment. It is to be assumed that relocation
assistance will be provided to those workers who lack the
financial resources to move to areas where employment is
available. Although a computerized job bank program can
overcome a lack of adequate information regarding manpower
needs, relocation assistance must be regarded as a logical
concomitant of such a program.

As was mentioned in Chapter 7, a national program of
relocation assistance could serve two different groups of
workers--unskilled or low-skilled workers, who are predominantly from rural areas, and well-trained industrial
workers who are displaced by mass layoffs. A different set
of services would be needed for each group. In the case of
workers from rural areas, extensive supportive services before and after relocation are essential. There would have to
be pre-move counseling and moving arrangements. Basic
education and extensive job training would also have to pre-
cede any attempt at relocation. Post-move counseling and
services would also have to be provided in order to aid relocatees in adapting to a new area. Greater success in relocation is assured when a coordinated program is available.
On the other hand, only relocation assistance is necessary
for unemployed workers who have had some industrial skills
and who are familiar with an urban environment.

The population of workers which would be eligible for relocation assistance could be rather large. For example, the
Department of Agriculture estimates that in the near future
200,000 jobs will vanish from the cultivation of tobacco, which
is now the largest user of farm labor in the country. In the
Mississippi Delta, a shift from human to mechanical methods
for picking cotton eliminated more than 50,000 agricultural
jobs in a five-county area--a short-term displacement which
was equal to the total number of all industrial jobs in the
Delta. Most of this displacement occurred in 1966 and 1967.

Estimates of the total population which a relocation program would serve can vary considerably. In 1968 an inter-agency work group representing the Bureau of the Budget, the Department of Labor, the Office of Economic Opportunity, and the Department of Health, Education, and Welfare estimated that 12. 3 million workers and potential workers aged 14 to 64 needed some form of manpower training or assistance. The largest groups which needed assistance were those residing in urban and rural poverty areas. This estimate, however, was limited only to poverty groups, and had nothing to do with industrial unemployment caused by factors unrelated to poverty.

The number of workers who would be eligible to receive relocation assistance is difficult to estimate. However, the population base from which relocatees would be selected is reduced considerably by the existence of various deficiencies which are difficult to overcome. Probably a majority of rural workers lack the basic educational and skill requirements necessary to make job training and relocation worthwhile. It is to be seriously doubted that much can be done with a person who has had a seventh- or eighth-grade education in a rural school, yet there are many thousands of these persons. The cultural isolation of rural disadvantaged groups is also difficult to overcome. For that matter, however, cultural isolation is not necessarily limited to persons who live in rural areas-- ghetto residents can also be affected.

The Canadian and Swedish national relocation programs have been used as a frame of reference. It has been pointed out that some 22, 000 workers received relocation allowances in Sweden during the fiscal year 1968-69. If this number were pro-rated in terms of the U. S. labor force, it would mean that some 500, 000 workers would receive relocation assistance. However, the comparison is not valid, for Sweden is a much more homogeneous country than the United States and possesses a higher literacy rate. Canada is less homogeneous than Sweden, in that there are two main languages, English and French. But Canada does not have the racial problems which tend to militate against labor mobility in the United States.

The Department of Labor has suggested a national relocation program which would start with the movement of

20, 000 workers a year. Based on the average cost of relocation for the experimental labor mobility projects, the
cost of such a relocation program would be around $150 million
a year. This includes administrative costs, which presumably
would be much less with a standardized national program. The
total cost, then, could be lowered to $100 million a year or
less. The number of relocations could be much larger as a
matter of national policy. However, everything would depend
upon the maintenance of effective demand for labor of the sort
that is in supply. This may be a rather difficult task to perform. It is also necessary that cheap and adequate housing
be available near the job. There is little in national policy
statements to indicate that cheap housing is a goal to be
attained.

Relocation assistance is not proposed as a panacea for
poverty, unemployment, and underemployment. It should be
a part of a wide range of manpower services, out of which
programs for particular localities or individuals can be adapted
to meet specific needs and opportunities. These services
would include adult education to remedy the deficiencies of
earlier schooling, subsidized private employment for the disadvantaged, creation of public service jobs for workers who
cannot be absorbed in the labor market, and relocation allowances for workers who can be placed in employment in labor
shortage areas. Other remedial manpower services would also be provided. Supportive services--such as counseling and
day-care centers for small children of working mothers--would
be provided for those who need corrective measures to secure
employment. Special inducements would be provided to attract
industry into depressed areas.

Relocation assistance has a place as part of a comprehensive national manpower program. Its major role should
be to induce not simply more outmigration, but a more rational
outmigration, and to facilitate a matching of workers and employment opportunities. By making relocation assistance contingent on a move to known employment opportunities, much
fruitless and unnecessary movement can be avoided. A poor
allocation among productive alternatives can cause otherwise
adequate resources to produce inadequate income. If investment in job training is to bear fruit in terms of job placement,
the relocation of trained workers, particularly those in depressed areas, will frequently be necessary. There also

appears to be some potential in relocating unskilled workers from rural areas, but there are problems which are very difficult to minimize. Relocation would provide no major solution to unemployment, but it would be important to those who took advantage of it.

Some economists have argued that the existence of a labor surplus in an area means relatively low wage costs, which could act to raise the marginal efficiency of investment. Therefore, capital should be attracted to such an area--if necessary, through the use of some type of incentive. This investment presumably leads to an increase in the demand for labor, unemployment declines, and some part of the increase in income induces investment in other activities. There are, of course, public sector effects as well. These take the form of increased investment in the area's public overhead capital. Total regional product and total regional income will increase as a result of the capital movement.

However, the most productive elements of the labor force usually migrate out of areas with few worthwhile employment opportunities, leaving behind a labor pool of diminished pro- ductive potential. If the residual labor force in a region is not of adequate quality to be combined with the type of capital that might migrate into the area, then the expected future earnings on investment will not be raised by the existence of surplus labor. Moreover, the new capital investment may stimulate an inmigration of labor. The inmigrants may be former residents who return with the expectation of gaining employment. Since they may have gained some industrial ex- perience elsewhere, they will probably be hired in preference to the area's unemployed and underemployed.

It is apparent that there might be some difficulty in desig- nating the working force population which would be eligible for relocation assistance. In recent years of high employment, about one-half of the workers who are unemployed in any one week have been out of work for less than five weeks, or a max- imum of about a month. In April, 1969, almost 1.4 million out of 2.5 million unemployed workers had been out of work for one month or less. The hardcore unemployed, who can be defined as those who have been out of work for 15 weeks or longer, amounted to some 500,000 workers. Unemployment insurance benefits are generally available for 26 weeks to those

workers covered by the system. In April, 1969, there were
160,000 workers who had been unemployed for more than 26
weeks. There are also persons who have been unemployed
so long that they have really dropped out of the labor force
and are no longer considered as unemployed.

When the marginally employed workers are added to the
unemployed, the potential population is larger than the entire
Swedish labor force. Obviously, some constraints are necessary. But, first of all, it is likely that the majority of this
population of underemployed and unemployed workers would
not possess the skill requirements to be absorbed into anything but the most rudimentary jobs. Thus, relocation assistance should involve workers who are unemployed in a labor
surplus area and for whom employment is available in other
areas. Preferably, some form of job training should accompany the use of relocation assistance. Although unemployment should be the basic criterion for receiving relocation
assistance, it might be desirable to extend the assistance to
workers who will become unemployed in the future and have
no prospects for immediate reemployment in the home area.

Economic growth and social progress inevitably result
in some mismatching of labor supply and demand. Job opportunities multiply in one region and disappear in another,
and new industries expand while old ones decline. Too often,
these changes create worker displacement and joblessness.
An active manpower policy can minimize these problems by
providing measures which would include occupational training
and retraining, improving the flow of information about manpower requirements, resources, and job opportunities, and
facilitating the movement of displaced workers from areas
where jobs are scarce to places where workers are scarce.
The view that in the free market, worker and job matches
will occur unassisted, overlooks the difference between an
efficient and an inefficient labor market. Specific labor shortages can slow up economic expansion and raise costs and
prices. Increasing the time required to place the right man
in the right job decreases the output of goods and services.
Policies which bring men and jobs together and increase the
productivity of the labor force are bound to redound to the
advantage of the economy.

NOTES

1.   Sar A. Levitan, <u>Federal Aid to Depressed Areas</u>
(Baltimore: The Johns Hopkins Press, 1964), p. 240.

2.   <u>Economic Report of the President </u>(1969), pp. 98-101.

3.   <u>Ibid</u>. , p. 178.

APPENDIXES

INTRODUCTION

Relocation assistance was provided in an amendment to the Manpower Development and Training Act, and was funded in three phases reflecting periodic extension of funds. Workers who were relocated had to be unemployed or underemployed and to have no reasonable expectation of employment in their home communities. An offer of a job in the demand or receiving area was required prior to relocation. The relocation projects that were in operation were diverse in nature, but most involved rural-to-urban shifts in employment. Some projects involved unemployed MDTA graduates; others involved unskilled workers from rural areas. Many persons expressed a willingness to relocate, but not all could be offered jobs. For most projects, the ratio of those who were willing to relocate to the actual number of persons relocated was 3 to 1. With more money and resources, the projects could have moved thousands of additional workers.

Four projects in Michigan, Mississippi, North Carolina, and West Virginia have been selected for the purpose of analyzing more closely the operation of the relocation program. These projects moved approximately one-fourth of all of the workers who received relocation assistance. The West Virginia project involved the relocation of workers from coal mining counties in the state to jobs in other states. The unemployed workers from which the relocatees were selected fell mainly into two groups: older workers who were displaced by automation in the coal industry, and young workers who recently entered the labor force. North Carolina and Mississippi had projects that were designed to discover and initiate communications with persons who were not fully employed either in agriculture or in other aspects of the rural economy. These persons were predominantly Negro, had a low level of educational attainment, and often had incomes of $1,200 or less a year. The projects attempted to identify those workers who could relocate to other areas and to provide counseling for them for a long enough period to implant the idea that there might be something better for them somewhere else. The fourth project was operated by Northern Michigan University. It was designed to relocate workers from depressed areas in northern Michigan to employment in industrial centers in the state and in Wisconsin.

Educational attainment and age are important determinants of the direction and magnitude of labor migration. Mobility increases with educational attainment and decreases with age because, given any difference in expected future earnings among regions, these differences are largest for the most educated and the youngest members of the labor force. To a lesser extent marital status, color, and property ownership have an influence on mobility. The number of dependents and property ownership act to reduce mobility, and nonwhites are somewhat less mobile than whites.

In evaluating the results of the labor mobility projects, it is necessary to remember that the methods of operation differed for each project. In the West Virginia project, the state employment service was responsible for relocation. Recruitment was done by out-of-state employers, and Travelers Aid provided supportive services. The Mississippi and North Carolina projects were similar in that private organizations were responsible for recruitment and placement of the relocatees, and for providing the necessary supportive services. The North Carolina project was the only one of the four which relocated workers exclusively within state boundaries. The projects were funded for either two or three stages. The North Carolina and West Virginia projects were two of the original projects that were started in 1965.

Personnel turnover on the projects was extremely high. The Mississippi project reported a 100 percent turnover in field workers during the period from the first stage of the project to the start of the second stage. This turnover of operating personnel is understandable because a high degree of uncertainty was associated with the re-funding of the projects. Nevertheless, the expertise gained from the operation of a project was often lost by the time it was re-funded for further operations.

The rate of return to the home area would have to be regarded as high. A successful relocation was operationally defined as occurring when a relocatee was still in the demand area two months after he had been relocated. A defect of the experimental relocation projects is that no attempt was made to see what had happened to the relocatees after an extended period of time. After the two-month follow-up period, contact was broken with the relocatees. Some of the first projects reported that as many as a third of all of the relocatees had returned home after two months had elapsed. This rate was reduced considerably as the projects moved into subsequent stages.

The labor mobility projects demonstrate that relocation can be used as a national program at a reasonable cost for certain unemployed segments of the population. Many workers are cast into the labor market to fend for themselves. In fact and theory, the labor market is still the principal mechanism for adjusting to manpower requirements. However, the labor market does not operate as efficiently as it should, and much effort on the part of workers to secure employment is wasted and misdirected. Relocation assistance can match workers with jobs, and can also provide a substantial improvement in money income. For example, a West Virginia labor mobility project reported an average income differential of more than $2,000 per relocatee between jobs before and after relocation. However, it is necessary to point out that this differential was narrowed to a certain extent by higher living costs in the areas to which the relocatees were sent.

APPENDIX THE WEST VIRGINIA
LABOR MOBILITY
PROJECTS

The West Virginia labor mobility demonstration projects
were designed to serve economically depressed counties in
the southwestern part of the state. The purpose of these projects was to relocate unemployed coal miners from an area
which has depended to a major degree on coal mining. The
economic dislocation in this area--which consists of Boone,
Fayette, Logan, McDowell, Mercer, Mingo, Raleigh, and
Wyoming counties--has been severe as a result of a precip-
itous decline in employment in coal mining.

The rate of unemployment in this area of West Virginia
has been among the highest in the nation over an extended
period of time. In 1958, when the national unemployment rate
was 6. 8 percent, the unemployment rate in Raleigh County was
24. 5 percent, and the unemployment rate in McDowell County
was 23. 5 percent. In 1968 the national unemployment rate had
declined to 3. 6 percent--the lowest rate since the end of the
Korean War. Unemployment rates in Raleigh and McDowell
counties had declined to 6. 2 and 8. 8 percent, respectively.
The unemployment rate for Fayette County was 9. 4 percent
and for Mingo County, 9. 8 percent. However, this decline in
the rate of unemployment can be attributed primarily to outmigration from these counties, rather than to national policies
designed to bring industry into the area. The total work force
in some of these counties has decreased by as much as 40 percent during the ten-year period. Although industry has been
attracted into the area, its overall effect on the creation of
employment opportunities is open to question.

The coal industry's importance as the prime creator
of all jobs--primarily or secondarily related to mining--
in this area cannot be overemphasized. In 1949, mining
employment alone was responsible for 78, 000 jobs, and
the area produced 57 percent of West Virginia's coal. Added
to the 78, 000 jobs were thousands of others which were
based on mining. Railroad employment in the area depended

upon the mining of coal, and employment in retailing and service areas also was contingent upon economic conditions in
the coal mining industry. Salaries for coal miners were
among the highest for all industrial workers in the United
States.

After 1949, the coal-mining industry was beset by a
number of problems, the first and most important of which
was a change in the method of mining underground coal.
Machines were developed which could do the job more expeditiously than by the use of labor. Simultaneous with this
technological shift which raised output relative to man-hours
was the transition of the railroads from steam to diesel loco-
motives, which lowered the railroads' coal consumption from
94 million tons in 1948 to such an insignificant amount in 1967
that data is no longer published by the West Virginia Department of Mines. Postwar recessions also contributed to the
decline in employment in coal mining. In each of the recovery
phases, only a portion of those workers who were unemployed
were ever recalled to employment.

The collective impact of these problems had an extremely
adverse effect on the eight-county area. Mining employment
declined from 78, 000 in 1949 to 25, 330 in 1966. This reduction was confined exclusively to men who were among the best-
paid of all production workers in the country, and who formed
the economic base of the area.

Unemployment in the area, which amounted to 5. 1 percent
in 1950, increased to 21. 6 percent in 1958 and 24 percent by
1960. On a county basis, the average unemployment rate in
1958 ranged from 9. 9 percent for Wyoming County to 28. 9
percent for Fayette County. In 1962, the average unemployment rate had declined to 18 percent for the eight counties.
Since 1962, there has been a decline in the unemployment rate
to an average of 9. 6 percent for 1966. It is necessary to point
out that this rate was more than twice the national average
unemployment rate for the year, and that the rate also varied
considerably by county. This latter fact is reflected in Table
24.

In 1961, the Kennedy administration passed the Area Redevelopment Act. Its purpose was to combat unemployment
and underemployment in the nation's economically distressed

TABLE 24

Unemployment Rates in Eight West Virginia Counties,
1958, 1962, 1966

County	1958	1962	1966
Boone	16.4%	19.9%	11.1%
Fayette	28.8	22.5	13.9
Logan	16.4	19.9	11.1
McDowell	23.5	20.6	10.8
Mercer	19.8	13.6	6.8
Mingo	28.2	22.9	13.9
Raleigh	24.5	16.9	7.4
Wyoming	9.9	9.4	5.4

Source: West Virginia Department of Employment Security.

areas. Specific measures provided included low-interest loans
to business firms locating in depressed areas and public works
facilities designed to improve the infrastructures of depressed
areas.

There has been a considerable amount of outmigration in
the area over the last 15 years, and it has been a key factor
in reducing the rate of unemployment. In 1950, the population
of the eight counties amounted to 548,129 persons. By 1964,
the population had declined to 408,500 persons. During the
period from 1960 to 1964, 35,000 persons left the area. Although the population has stabilized since about 1965, it is
apparent that prospects for the future will continue to depend
to a considerable degree on developments in coal mining. In
the last several years there has been some increase in coal
mining activity; however, continued technological change has
resulted in a qualitative upgrading of jobs in mining, and many
people will be forced to go out of the area to find employment.

Table 25 presents changes in the labor force and in the
number of unemployed workers for Boone and Logan counties
over a ten-year period. It is significant to note that increases
in employment in manufacturing were modest during this period. In 1958, 620 persons were employed in manufacturing
in the two counties; in 1967, the number was 940. However,
the number of persons employed in manufacturing was stabilized at around that number for the period 1963-67, indicating
that gains in employment in this area had no effect in reducing
the rate of unemployment. Employment in coal mining stabilized at around 7,000 workers for the period 1961-67--a reduction of more than 10,000 since the peak period after the
Second World War.

Constant lay-offs and a lack of employment opportunities
have created a concomitant problem of poverty in the area.
According to the 1960 census report, of the 103,683 families
in the area, 40,297 (38.9 percent) reported family incomes
of less than $3,000 a year. In 1965, 48 percent of all wage
earners in the eight counties had incomes of less than $3,000. [1]
A percentage breakdown of families making less than $3,000
a year is presented in Table 26.

In summary, the following points can be made about this
eight-county coal mining area in southwestern West Virginia:

TABLE 25

Work Force and Unemployment Rates, Boone and Logan Counties,
1958-67

Year	Work Force	Unemployed	Unemployment Rate
1958	26,450	4,350	16.4%
1959	25,260	4,460	17.7
1960	23,270	4,030	17.0
1961	22,000	4,720	21.4
1962	21,210	4,220	19.9
1963	20,870	3,590	17.2
1964	20,500	3,160	15.4
1965	20,380	2,880	14.1
1966	19,940	2,260	11.3
1967	20,000	2,240	11.1

Source: Research and Statistics Division, West Virginia Department of
Employment Security, Statistical Handbook, 1958-1967, pp. 10, 11.

207

TABLE 26

Families with Incomes of Less Than $3,000 a Year in Eight West
Virginia Counties, 1960

County	Percent
Boone	39.8
Fayette	41.0
Logan	32.6
McDowell	41.4
Mercer	36.8
Mingo	46.1
Raleigh	39.9
Wyoming	33.6

Source: West Virginia Department of Employment Security.

1.   The unemployment rate has been among the highest for any area in the nation for the last 15 years. Even though the unemployment rate at present is less than half of the rate eight years ago, it is still more than twice the national average.

2.   The level of poverty, expressed in terms of a departure from a minimum level of income, is high in comparison with the state as a whole. This situation can be attributed to prolonged unemployment and a lack of job opportunities in the area.

3.   While federal programs, such as the Appalachian Redevelopment Program, may have some impact on the economy of the area, it may be years until their effect can be realized. Certainly it is necessary that long-term programs for persons residing in these counties be designed to create employment. However, in the short term, prospects are unfavorable, and it would be a waste of human resources to try to retain people in the area until conditions improve, particularly if available jobs are going begging elsewhere.

RELOCATION OF UNEMPLOYED WORKERS

There were three labor mobility demonstration projects in West Virginia that extended over the period 1965 to 1968. Relocatees were selected primarily from the southwestern counties of the state, where many jobs had been made obsolete by technological advances in the coal industry. In the first project, relocation was from the coal mining counties of Logan, McDowell, Mercer, and Wyoming to out-of-state jobs secured by the West Virginia Department of Employment Security.

Out of 466 workers found eligible for relocation allowances, 225 expressed a willingness to move. Seventy-five workers were moved to out-of-state jobs. (The workers, all male, were placed in Maryland (34), New York (24), Virginia (6), Michigan (6), Indiana (3), New Jersey (1), and Illinois (1) at wages ranging from $1.16 to $3.46 an hour, two-thirds of them earning between $1.67 and $2.10 an hour. Only three had job training under the Manpower Development Training Act prior to the move; 40 had less than nine years of education; and 23 were over 40 years old.) All but one received re- location allowances. The total cost of the allowances was $10,137. The average cost of a relocation, exclusive of ad- ministrative costs, was less than $150. This was considerably lower than anticipated, and reflected the fact that 30 of the 75 workers were single.

All of the workers had been unemployed before the re- location. Thirty-seven had been unemployed 52 weeks or longer prior to the move; eight had been unemployed for 26 to 52 weeks; eight had been unemployed from 15 to 26 weeks; and the remainder had been unemployed for less than 15 weeks.

The rate of return to the home area was high. Thirty-six, or approximately half, of the relocatees returned to the home area within a year after the move. Several factors can be cited for this high rate of return.

1.   Higher living costs in the area of relocation was one problem. Eighteen of the 34 workers located in Maryland returned to the home area. The average hourly wage for the relocatees in Maryland was $1.67. Employment was in canning factories in the Chesapeake Bay area. Most of the men who returned from Maryland were married, and it is apparent that living costs, on a salary of about $67 a week, discouraged them from remaining in the new place of employment.

2.   The transition from a rural mountain environment to an entirely new environment was an inhibiting factor which was responsible for the high rate of return. This, however, can be attributed in part to a lack of provision for extensive social services both before and after the move.

3.   There was also a relationship between the average length of unemployment before moving to the new area and the rate of return. Twenty-two of the 37 workers who were un- employed for a year or longer returned to the home area.

The second labor mobility demonstration project broadened its sphere of operations to include four more West Virginia counties--Boone, Fayette, Mingo and Raleigh--which were ad- jacent to the original four counties. All of the counties were similar in that they had vast numbers of displaced coal miners.

The format of the second project differed from the first in two aspects:

1. Financial assistance was changed from a half-loan, half-grant basis to a 100 percent loan which could be converted into a 100 percent grant, provided that the worker remained on his job in the new area for a stipulated period of time. The obvious purpose of this new feature was to provide an incentive for the worker to remain in the new area or, conversely, a disincentive to return to the home area because the loan would have to be repaid. However, if the worker could provide a legitimate reason for returning to the home area, the loan provision was not put into effect.

2. Social guidance and counseling were provided to the relocatees both before and after the move through a contractural arrangement with Travelers Aid. It was felt that the transition to a new environment was a traumatic experience for many relocatees. If they could be assisted in the adjustment to an entirely new set of relations, the rate of return to the home area would be reduced. The importance of a rural-urban transition cannot be minimized; the success of a relocation program depends on the adaptation of workers to a situation which is different from that to which they have become accustomed.

During the period in which the project was in operation, 1,940 persons were screened for eligibility by the West Virginia Department of Employment Security. Requisites for eligibility were unemployment and lack of job opportunities in the home area. Out of 1,568 who were found eligible, 1,518 expressed a willingness to move, and 568 received relocation allowances. To find and screen workers who would be willing to relocate, six full-time interviewers were employed by the local Employment Security office in the area. The population consisted of workers who possessed various characteristics-- MDTA graduates, welfare recipients, and unemployment insurance beneficiaries. Contacts with potential relocatees were usually made through advertising of relocation assistance in the local newspapers; and through referrals of welfare recipients by local Department of Welfare offices.

Job placement was done by local Employment Security offices through telephone contacts with Employment Security

offices in other states, and through employer recruitment
efforts in the area. Some employers had recruited workers
during the first labor mobility project and apparently were
satisfied with their work. Other employers either had recruited in the area on previous occasions, or had had occasion
to employ workers who had left the area. Most job offers came
from employers who recruited in the area.

Relocation assistance included a travel allowance which
was designed to defray the cost of transporting a worker and
members of his family to the new place of employment; a lump-
sum allowance to defray the cost of living at the new place of
employment; a household goods allowance to cover the cost of
transporting furniture and other household items to the new
place of residence; and a temporary storage allowance to cover
the cost of temporary storage of household goods. Assistance
was provided on the basis of a loan which was convertible to
a grant, provided that the worker remained in the new place of
employment for 180 days. If the worker returned to the home
area, the loan had to be repaid; however, if he changed employment in the place of relocation and remained the required
period of time, the loan became a grant.

The amount of the travel allowance was based on the type
of transportation used. If transportation was by commercial
carrier, a travel allowance equal to the cost of the cheapest
public conveyance was provided for the worker and his family.
This meant that bus was invariably the method of public transportation. If a privately owned automobile was used, the worker
was compensated at the rate of 10 cents a mile. If the family
traveled by privately owned automobile at a time subsequent
to the time the worker traveled, the same rate was in effect.

The lump-sum allowance was payable to the relocatee and
his wife at a rate of $108 for both. If the relocatee was single,
he received a lump-sum allowance of $108. The amount of the
allowance was equal to the national average weekly wage during
the time of the move. If separate maintenance was necessary
until housing could be obtained in the new area, a lump-sum
payment of $54 a week was provided to each member of the
worker's family for a period of four weeks.

Relocation allowances were given to 568 persons. The
total cost of the assistance amounted to $208,806, and the

average cost of relocation per person amounted to $368.   The
relocatees were sent to 20 states and the District of Columbia.
The states receiving the most relocatees were Connecticut
(195), Michigan (54), Virginia (52), Wisconsin (48), Indiana
(47), Illinois (28), Pennsylvania (27), and Ohio (20).   Employers
providing employment were Pratt and Whitney in Connecticut
(173), Ford in Michigan (49), General Tire in Indiana (44),
Firestone in Virginia (38), and Grede Foundries in Wisconsin
(22).   The great majority of jobs were unskilled.   Relocation
was in areas with job shortages brought about by defense contracts for the Vietnam War.   At the end of April, 1967, 13
months after the project began, 163 of the relocations had been
termed unsuccessful because the relocatee had returned to the
home area or had not shown up at the place of employment.
There is no reason to doubt that the number of unsuccessful
relocations will continue to increase.   It is necessary to remember that the project extended over a 13-month period, and
that data presented includes only the number of unsuccessful
relocations during that period.

The most important characteristics of the relocatees are
age, education, and length of unemployment prior to the move.
The average age of the relocatee was 28, the average education
was 10 years, and the average length of unemployment was 26
weeks.   Table 27 presents the age characteristics of the successful and unsuccessful relocatees.   The term "successful"
means simply that the relocatee was employed in the area to
which he was sent at the time the project was completed--the
end of April, 1967.

There is a definite correlation between age and unsuccessful relocation.   The rate of unsuccessful relocations was considerably higher among workers in the older age groups.   It is
apparent that older workers are more attached to the home
area and find it more difficult to sever the umbilical cord.
This is not surprising.   European labor mobility programs
indicate a similar pattern.

There is also a correlation between the length of unemployment and the rate of unsuccessful relocations.   Workers
who were unemployed for a short period of time prior to the
relocation were much more likely to relocate successfully
than workers who had been unemployed for a longer period of
time.   To many workers who were unemployed for a

TABLE 27

Age of Relocatees in the West Virginia Labor Mobility Project

Age	All	Successful Relocatees	Unsuccessful Relocatees
19 and under 20	89	70	19
20 and under 25	173	129	44
25 and under 35	175	123	52
35 and under 45	103	65	38
45 and under 55	26	17	9
55 and under 65	2	1	1
	568	405	163

Source: West Virginia Department of Employment Security.

214

considerable period of time, welfare benefits provided an attractive alternative to working in a new area for a wage that was not much higher than the welfare benefit. Also, work habits and patterns tended to deteriorate if the worker was unemployed for a long period of time.

Table 28 presents a breakdown of the relocatees on the basis of the duration of unemployment. Some of the workers had job retraining under various programs sponsored under the Area Redevelopment Act and Manpower Development and Training Act. Most, however, did not receive training prior to the move. There was no relationship between the success or lack of success of relocation and the extent of job training prior to the move.

There was also a relationship between the time spent at the new place of employment and the success of the relocation. The majority of unsuccessful relocations took place during the first month in the new area: 32 percent of the relocatees returned to the home area within a week after relocation, and 24 percent returned within two to four weeks. Only 7 percent of the relocatees returned to the home area after a period of four months or longer had elapsed. This would indicate that the success of any relocation program could be enhanced considerably by the provision of social services during the initial, or critical, phase of the relocation. Workers, especially those from rural areas, need guidance in becoming socially and physically adjusted to new areas.

Pre-migration counseling was provided by Travelers Aid. However, the extent of the supply area created considerable problems. The eight county area is 300 miles from north to south and 135 miles from east to west. A major portion of the area covered by the social service counselors involved travel over mountains by secondary roads and footpaths. Home visits were often impeded by seasonal snows and floods. The time factor made more than one home visit unrealistic in most instances.

The provision of social services in the demand, or receiving, areas was difficult to accomplish because relocatees were sent to a number of states. There was a lack of coordination between social agencies in the supply and demand areas which was attributable in part to a time lag involved in

TABLE 28

Length of Unemployment of West Virginia Relocatees

Weeks Unemployed	Successful Relocatees	Unsuccessful Relocatees
0 and under 5	70	19
5 and under 15	129	44
15 and under 26	123	52
27 and under 52	65	38
52 and over	17	9
	1	1
	405	163

Source: West Virginia Department of Employment Security.

ascertaining whether or not post-migration social services
would be made available.

As mentioned previously, 163 workers were termed
"unsuccessful" relocatees at the completion date of the project. This term is misleading to a certain extent. Thirty-
nine relocatees were judged to have returned to the home area
for good reasons--lack of suitable housing in the demand area,
illness, change in draft status, and a cessation of employment.
Two workers died before becoming successfully relocated. For
the 122 workers whose relocation was determined as unsuccessful without good cause, the most important reason for
leaving the demand area was dislike for the job and the new
environment. A higher cost of living was also an important
factor.

Among relocatees who were termed "successful," there
was a high turnover rate which resulted from dislike of either
the job or the area. Of 110 workers who changed jobs after
relocation, 35 changed jobs within the same demand areas and
75 moved outside of the demand areas for employment. The
important point, however, is that many workers were able
to exercise initiative by moving to other areas to obtain employment.

Unlike the European relocation programs, workers were
not given the opportunity to visit demand areas and employers
prior to relocation. It may well be that the number of successful relocations would be substantially increased if workers
were afforded a chance to see the new area prior to moving.

The third labor mobility project was extended to include
the entire state, but concentration was placed mainly on the
relocation of workers from the coal mining counties. The recruiting procedures were the same as for the preceding projects, and Travelers Aid was used extensively in the provision
of both pre-move and post-move supportive services. A total
of 812 workers were relocated, and 776 received relocation
assistance. Most relocatees were sent to jobs in other states,
with Virginia receiving more than one-third of them. The
average amount of relocation assistance was $329, and the
average administrative cost per relocatee was $210. Admin-
istrative costs were affected by the starting and stopping of
the project on two separate occasions. Had the project

continued uninterrupted, staff time could have been utilized to greater advantage.

The average annual income of the 812 relocatees prior to relocation was $2,792. This is based on the assumption that they were fully employed for the year--an assumption which is obviously false, since unemployment was the basic criterion for receiving relocation assistance. In fact, 150 relocatees had been unemployed for 52 weeks or longer prior to relocation and had earned no income. The majority of relocatees were unemployed for a period of 26 weeks or longer. The average projected annual income after relocation was $4,819. This assumes that all of the relocatees remained employed a year after relocation--an assumption which is also not valid. Nevertheless, there is no question that the overall monetary gain from relocation is considerable. One-third of the relocatees were placed in jobs which paid an income of $5,000 or more a year. Many relocatees had received some type of MDTA job training before relocation, and were placed as auto mechanics, machinists, welders, and electricians in jobs in other states.

After the standard two-month follow-up period, 138 relocatees had left the demand areas, and 115 had returned home. The most important reason for unsuccessful relocation was the lack of suitable housing. Also, an undetermined number of workers were not relocated because of inadequate housing in some of the demand areas, and only single workers were sent to jobs in other areas because suitable housing was not available for families. Higher living costs in the demand areas was also a reason why many relocatees returned home.

SUMMARY

The purpose of the West Virginia labor mobility projects was to assist unemployed workers from the coal mining area of the state in relocating in other states where employment was available. This area had sustained above-average unemployment rates for two decades, and efforts to attract industry had not been particularly successful. The level of poverty in the area is high, and many persons are on the welfare rolls.

During the period in which the projects were in effect, 1,455 persons were relocated. The demand areas were widely scattered. All but a few relocatees were moved out of the state. The form of relocation assistance was a loan, which was converted to a grant if the worker remained in the area of employment for a prescribed period of time. The assistance consisted of a travel allowance, a family allowance, and an allowance for the removal and storage of household possessions.

Local Employment Security offices in the supply area had the responsibility for screening and selecting the relocatees. Six full-time interviewers were assigned to coordinate the recruiting and selection of relocatees. The population from which the relocatees were selected included unemployment insurance claimants, welfare recipients, and MDTA training graduates. Unemployment was the basic criterion for relocation.

Workers selected for relocation were undoubtedly those who were rated as having the best chance for success. In essence, the "cream of the crop" was selected. However, most of those persons who were screened for eligibility indicated a willingness to move if relocation assistance was provided.

The following tentative conclusions can be made concerning the project:

1.   A number of workers were willing to move with relocation assistance. To a certain extent, this negates the belief that workers from mountain or rural areas are immobile and will not leave their environment. However, the rate of return to the home area was high, indicating that the transition from a rural to an urban environment was a traumatic experience for many workers.

2.   The turnover at the new place of employment was high. Many workers left their jobs to obtain other jobs within or outside of the demand area. However, this in itself was salutary, in that workers were more mobile after their basic ties with their home areas were severed.

3.   The rate of return to the home area can be reduced through the provision of a more comprehensive screening process, and through provision of counseling services in the demand area.   The number of returns to the home area cannot be judged an unqualified failure because many workers return with new skills and are able to obtain jobs in the home area.

B

The Department of Labor contracted with the North Carolina Fund to conduct several labor mobility demonstration projects designed to move workers from rural counties into more prosperous areas of the state. Probably the most outstanding positive feature of the projects is that they have attempted to reach the rural, unskilled, unemployed, or low-income worker who has not been touched by other social welfare programs, and to provide him with employment opportunities.

North Carolina has a rather diverse economy. In the industrialized Piedmont area, the unemployment rate has been low and the state has been making rapid strides in promoting the development of industry. However, there are rural agricultural regions where the decline of agriculture, coupled with a lack of industrialization, has depressed the local economies. Automation on tobacco and cotton farms has displaced many workers. North Carolina is the leading tobacco-producing state, and the leveling off in national tobacco consumption caused by the health reports on smoking is expected to cause a loss of some 100,000 jobs in the tobacco industry by 1975.

Disparities in employment opportunities in North Carolina counties are reflected in wide variations in per capita incomes. For example, in Mecklenburg County (Charlotte), per capita personal income in 1966 was $3,299. In Hyde County, the per capita personal income for 1966 was $1,143. In Guilford County, (Greensboro), the per capita personal income was $3,078: In Gates County, it was $1,156. The per capita income for the state was $2,277 in 1966--a rather low income when compared with the per capita income of $3,777 for the United States. Twenty-five of the 100 North Carolina counties had per capita incomes of $1,500 or less.[2]

Unemployment rates in North Carolina for 1967 ranged from a high of 12.5 percent for Camden County to 1.7 percent in Cabarrus County. Graham County had an unemployment rate of 11.6 percent, and Clay County had an unemployment rate of 10.1 percent.[3] Several counties had unemployment rates in excess of 9 percent. The average unemployment rate for the state in 1967 was 3.2 percent.

RELOCATION

In June, 1965, the Department of Labor contracted with the North Carolina Fund to conduct a mobility demonstration project to move several hundred workers--mainly poorly educated and low-skilled Negroes and Indians--from six rural eastern counties into more prosperous areas of the state. The counties involved were Craven, Edgecombe, Nash, Richmond, Robeson, and Scotland. The unemployment rate in these counties ranged from 5.9 percent to 12.5 percent. With the exception of Robeson County, the counties were not among the poorest in the state. Most of the workers moved were not unemployed, but were in the eligible category of members of farm families with a yearly income of under $1,200.

Financial assistance to the relocatees consisted of a lump-sum relocation allowance ranging from $51.50 for a single person with no dependents up to a maximum of $178, plus one-half of the moving costs. This sum could be matched with an equal amount in the form of an interest-free loan.

The first relocation project was completed in September, 1965. A total of 278 workers were moved at a cost of $32,062.[4] A large majority were single Negroes or Indians, although some families were moved. Almost 200 were employed in the textile and furniture industries in the Piedmont region. High Point, a furniture manufacturing town, received 120 of the workers. In High Point, the North Carolina Fund rented an apartment building and turned it into a temporary residence for the relocatees, who paid $13 a month for room and board.

Seventy percent of the workers receiving relocation allowances were males. The age range was 18 to 63, although

the majority were under 30. Seventeen percent were illiterate.
The starting salaries in the new jobs to which the relocatees
moved ranged from $1.25 to $2.59 an hour, with the majority
earning nearer the lower end of this range.[5]

The results of the first relocation project were both positive and negative. On the positive side, the income of the
average worker who was relocated was considerably larger
than it was in the home area. Two months after relocation,
the average worker was earning an income of $1.59 an hour,
which was equivalent to $3,300 a year, compared with an in-
come of $1,200 or less in the home area. Even when such
factors as imputed rent and income in kind, which can reduce
the differential between a cash farm income of $1,200 and an
income of $3,300 in the urban areas, are considered, the
differential still remained large.

Instability of employment on the part of the relocatees
was a negative factor. A year after the project ended, only
26 percent of the relocatees remained in their original jobs
or were still in the demand or receiving area. Eleven percent had left North Carolina to seek employment in other
states, while 32 percent had secured employment in the home
area. Of the remaining 31 percent of the relocatees, 9 percent had been drafted, 14 percent were unemployed in the
home area, 3 percent were farming, and 5 percent were in
school or elsewhere.

However, the high rate of return to the home area cannot
in itself be considered an indication of failure. Actually, the
work habits and new experience gained on the job served as
sort of a training program and made the workers more desirable in terms of employment in the home area.

A preliminary cost-benefit analysis indicated that the
total cost of moving workers could be recouped in one year.[6]
Estimates made from samples of workers who were successfully relocated and of workers who returned home indicated
that the total gain in earnings more than offset the total cost
of relocation, including forgone earnings, within a year. The
returns to the individuals involved exceeded the cost of relocation within a year. This is a very high rate of return on an
investment in human capital or, for that matter, in any type
of capital. Even though it ignores the psychic costs involved

in leaving an area, the return probably is far superior to the returns on a program designed to bring industry into an area.

The second North Carolina labor mobility project was started in March, 1966, and completed in September, 1967. The original six-county supply area was expanded to 42 counties. These counties were located in the Appalachian region of the state as well as in the eastern coastal region. The counties were designated as low-income counties, using the poverty income criterion of $3,000 a year set by the Council of Economic Advisers. For example, in Alleghany County, 51.3 percent of all families in 1959 had incomes of less than $3,000 a year, and for other counties, such as Greene and Clay, the rate was considerably higher. In Clay County, 70.9 percent of all families had incomes of less than $3,000 a year, and in Greene County the percentage was 70.3. The average for the state was 37.3 percent.[7]

Moreover, a deficit of more than 110,000 jobs was projected for the 42-county area by 1970. In Johnston County alone, a deficit of 11,700 was expected to occur by 1970.[8] Many of the counties lacked transportation, industry, and mineral resources. In some of the counties, as much as 70 percent of the families were tenant farmers. These projections were made in 1965, before the tobacco industry in the state was beginning to feel the effects of public campaigns against smoking. At the same time, a surplus of new jobs was projected for many North Carolina counties by 1970. For example, in Mecklenburg County (Charlotte), a surplus of 21,000 jobs was projected by 1970, and a surplus of 17,000 jobs was projected for Guilford County (Greensboro).[9] A total surplus of around 100,000 new jobs was forecast for some of the more developed counties in the state.

The deficit of jobs existed in the agricultural coastal plain counties and in the mountain counties of the Appalachian region. The surplus of jobs existed primarily in the rapidly developing Piedmont area of the state. Although a high demand for production workers existed in such cities as High Point, Greensboro, and Charlotte, certain factors worked against the successful mobility of workers from problem areas in the state. For one thing, many workers from the rural areas are uneducated and unskilled. To a certain extent this can be remedied through job training. This, however,

would come too late for many. Equally important are a col-
lection of attitudes which are difficult to break--apathy, a
sense of dependency upon the home environment, and a dis-
trust and fear of the "outside" world, even though employment
is available a few counties away.

The amount of relocation benefits and the form of recruitment were varied to some extent. Eligibility for relocation
assistance was still limited to unemployed workers or workers
from farms with cash income of less than $1,200 a year. Age
requirements were set at a minimum of 18 years and a maximum of 45 years. Recruitment of potential relocatees was
based on personal contacts--the recruiters went out into the
supply areas looking for persons who were willing to relocate.
Pre-relocation counseling was provided to explain the advantages of relocation to workers and their families. Receiving
and supportive services were also improved.

The second North Carolina labor mobility project moved
489 persons during the period from March, 1966, to September, 1967. A total of 6,545 persons were screened for relocation. In general, those persons who were relocated were
untrained, and were either unemployed for six weeks or more
or had incomes of $1,200 a year or less. Of the 489 relo-
catees, all but one were relocated in North Carolina. The
relocatees were sent primarily to the cities of Statesville,
Lexington, High Point, Charlotte, and Greensboro, and were
employed mostly in the textile, furniture, construction, and
steel industries. The relocatees numbered 412 males, and
77 females. The great majority of the relocatees were either
Negroes or Indians. The average cost of relocation, excluding
administrative costs, was $171, and the average distance
moved was 150 miles.

Certain factors exist, particularly in the rural coastal
counties of eastern North Carolina, which tend to prevent a
more successful relocation program in terms of the number
of workers that could be potentially moved. Tenant farmers
and farm laborers, who would make up the bulk of potential
relocatees, are in debt to their employers throughout most of
the year. They are under an obligation to remain with the
employers or landlords until after harvest time, when accounts
are settled and debts paid off. Many tenant farmers remain in
debt to the landlord or to storekeepers. A sense of dependency

develops on the part of the farmer, for often the landlord is the only person to whom he can turn for credit. Also, in the rural areas, housing is usually rent-free, meaning that it is provided by the landlord in return for services rendered on the land.

Another factor which is of paramount importance in relocation is the attachment of many persons to the home area or community. This attachment is particularly prevalent in the rural coastal counties, and was the major factor cited by many persons for not wanting to move, even to cities within the state and within relatively easy commuting distances from the home area. There is a dependency upon family and relatives, and upon interpersonal ties, that is difficult to break. A series of ties provides a sense of assurance and security to these rural persons, although economic insecurity brought about by the vicissitudes of farming and by automation marks the lot of most. It would appear that some sort of public works program might be feasible in order to provide employment for some of these workers, but this would, at best, provide only a partial solution to the problem of rural unemployment of underemployment.

Reluctance to leave on the part of many, however, does not preclude the use of relocation assistance, for obviously there are those who would leave if given the opportunity to do so. The population from which potential relocatees can be selected is large in North Carolina--numbering at least several hundred thousand.

The second North Carolina project used only grants, the amount of which depended upon the size of the family. For single persons, a flat grant of $75 was made to cover the costs of transportation and settling in. Families received a grant which covered settling-in expenses, the moving of household goods and the family, and separate maintenance of the family in the supply area until the relocatee found housing in the demand area. This grant was of two types. One provided $150 for the head of the household and spouse, $50 for each additional dependent up to a maximum of five, and $10 for each additional dependent. Moving expenses and the separate maintenance allowance were based on actual costs. The second type of grant provided $150 for the household head and spouse, $60 for the first five dependents, and $20 for each additional dependent. A flat sum of $100 was provided for transportation and for removal of household belongings.

Most of the 489 persons who were relocated were untrained, and had been unemployed for six weeks or more. Their level of educational attainment was low compared with national averages, but was about average for the rural South. About half of the relocatees had less than a 10th grade education, but 120 had finished high school.[10] However, rural youth are generally poorly educated, regardless of the years of educational attainment. This lag in education is even greater in those regions characterized by a high proportion of poor families. Census data indicate that educational expenditures per pupil tend to vary inversely with the percent of the total population which is rural. This is true even though a larger proportion of these expenditures must be made for transportation. So those persons who were relocated in North Carolina were laboring under the handicap of having a poor basic education. Furthermore, it is necessary to remember that more than 90 percent of them were Negroes and Indians. Although the quality of rural education is generally poor, there is a definite dichotomy of quality between rural white and rural colored schools, with the latter being inferior to the former. It is likely, then, that those relocatees who had finished high school in the rural areas had the equivalent of an eighth- or ninth-grade education when compared with urban youths.

Only 41 of the 489 relocatees had any form of savings prior to moving. This illustrates the point that moving on your own can be rather difficult without any savings. The total family income of 71 percent of the relocatees was less than $1,200 in the year prior to relocation, but only a small percent were on welfare.[11]

The results of relocation can be considered mixed. The project demonstrated that many workers from a rural environment are willing to move if provided the opportunity, and it also demonstrated that in terms of derived monetary benefits, compared with the cost of relocation, the gain can be significant if workers remain on their jobs or obtain similar jobs in the demand area. However, it can be established that a number of relocatees left their jobs to return to the home area, or for other reasons. Out of 453 workers moved, 219 had left their job within six months after the move. (The administrative definition of a successful relocation was employment in the demand area for a period of two months.) Half of these workers returned to the home area. Some of the others quit to take another job in the relocation area or outside of the state.

Charles Fairchild made a study of the second project, with the purpose of testing the effectiveness of relocation assistance in improving the opportunities of disadvantaged rural workers. The study attempted to find the answers to four basic questions:

1. Can the migration of the rural poor be channeled in more rational directions?

2. Does subsidized relocation result in permanent shifts in the population?

3. Do those who receive relocation assistance experience employment and earnings gains compared with persons who remain in the home area or those who move without relocation assistance?

4. Is relocation assistance an efficient technique in the sense of gains exceeding costs?

To answer these and other questions, Fairchild took a test group and a control group. The test group consisted of workers who had received relocation assistance, and the control group consisted of workers who had received no assistance. Both groups possessed the same basic characteristics and were from the same area. Interviews of both groups were made at the time of relocation for the test group, and follow-up interviews were made later. A comparison was made of the mobility of both groups to ascertain whether or not the relocation assistance was given to persons who would have moved anyway. Relocation assistance had a favorable impact on migration. When the control group was interviewed a year after selection, 20 percent had left the home area. After the last follow-up interview for the group that received relocation assistance, 52 percent were living in the demand area.[12]

However, the follow-up periods differed in length.   A
projection was made of the number of relocatees who could be
expected to remain in the original demand area a year after
relocation, and an estimate of 33. 6 percent was developed.[13]
This is not far above the 20 percent of the control group who
moved without relocation.   However, there is one significant
factor which has to be considered.   The relocation project re-
directed migration into useful channels.   Relocations were
made within the state where jobs were available.   Arrangements were made for housing, supportive services were provided, and efforts were made to smooth the transition from a
rural to an urban environment.   These persons had shown
little or no mobility prior to relocation.   Tabulation of their
lifetime mobility showed that at the time of relocation 59 percent were living in the community in which they had been born,
and most of these had never lived anywhere else.   In fact, 10
percent of the relocatees had never been out of their home
county, and most had never left the state.

The overall effect of relocation in terms of income gain
can be summarized in Table 29, which presents family incomes before and after the relocation.   Although the gain in
income after relocation appears considerable, some dis-
counting has to be made.   First of all, after-relocation income assumes that the relocatees remained on the job for a
year.   The majority did not.   Also, the direct income payments expressed in the table do not take into consideration
other costs which would tend to reduce the differential.   Most
of those in the control group who moved left the state.   The
typical migration pattern out of the rural areas in North Carolina is to the major cities on the eastern seaboard--New York,
Philadelphia, and Baltimore.   Those who move usually are
ill-equipped to find jobs, and many end up unemployed and
compound the problems of the urban slums.

Employment gains were made by relocatees who stayed
in the demand area in comparison with those who left the demand area and those persons who were in the control group.
At the time of the follow-up interviews, 95 percent of the relocatees in the demand area were employed, compared with
80 percent of those persons in the control group who had moved
of their own volition.   Only 63. 8 percent of the relocatees who
left the demand area to return home or move elsewhere were
employed, compared with 70 percent of the control group who

TABLE 29

Family Income of North Carolina Relocatees
Before and After Relocation

Income	Number
Before relocation	
Under $1,200	320
1,200 and under 3,000	120
3,000 and under 5,000	7
*	6
	453
After relocation	
Under $1,200	6
1,200 and under 3,000	215
3,000 and under 5,000	229
5,000 and over	3
	453

*Information not available.

Source: Virginia Employment Commission. (Final reports of all relocation projects were sent to the Virginia Employment Commission for tabulation).

had remained in the home area.[14] Estimated average weekly
wages of all relocatees before relocation was $39.13; and es-
timated average weekly wages after relocation was $63.60--
a net gain of $24.47. The estimated average weekly earnings
for the control group, including those who left the supply area,
was $34.56, and $43.16 after the follow-up period.[15] In terms
of average annual earnings, relocatees who remained in the
demand area had a projected earnings gain of 122 percent
over their annual average wage prior to relocation. However,
relocatees who returned to the home area had a worse employment and earnings record than those persons who never
left the home area.

The study has several conclusions:[16]

1. Relocation has an enormous potential for increasing
the output and earnings of rural disadvantaged workers in
North Carolina, particularly if they remain in the demand
area. The implication is that a national program of relocation
assistance should concentrate in part on helping relocate rural
workers in general. There is a potential earnings gain which
results from increased employment and from higher earnings
per unit of time employed.

2. Job training in the demand area is needed to improve
the conditions of employment and income.

3. Although the second North Carolina labor mobility
project cannot be called an unqualified success, it demonstrated that assisted relocation can play an important role in
reducing poverty among the rural poor.

However, the question of real versus apparent money income differences arises from the magnitude of the returnee
problem. The fact that at least 50 percent of those who receive relocation assistance return to the home area within a
year after relocation means that the real and psychic costs
of leaving home must be balanced against the receipt of a
higher money income in the demand area. If the real income
difference is smaller than the apparent money income difference, the cost of not staying in the demand area is less, and
returning to the home area for any reason at all carries with
it a smaller penalty than otherwise would normally be the
case. When the psychic satisfaction of living in a familiar

environment is added to lower living costs in the home area,
it is apparent that the differential in income between the home
and demand areas is narrowed considerably.

THIRD NORTH CAROLINA
LABOR MOBILITY PROJECT

The third labor mobility project operated from October,
1967, through September, 1968. An additional 371 workers
were moved with relocation assistance. The recruiting or
supply area included the 30 eastern rural coastal counties
and the 12 mountain counties used in the previous relocation
project. The eligibility requirements were unchanged. Farm
families with incomes of $1,200 a year or less, and workers
unemployed for a period of six weeks or longer, were eligible
for relocation assistance. A total of 3,989 workers were
screened for relocation, and 11 recruiters, each responsible
for three to six counties, were responsible for searching for
potential relocatees. The population from which the relocatees
were selected consisted for the most part of unskilled workers.

Some changes were made in relocation procedures. In
the first and second mobility projects, the majority of the
relocatees had left the demand area within a year after relocation. To reduce this loss, more supportive services were
added. Boarding houses were provided for relocatees until
housing could be found. Closer contact was maintained with
the relocatees by those who were responsible for the operation
of the relocation program. Pre-relocation counseling was
also used in the selection process.

Relocation assistance amounted to a flat $115 for all
single workers. This amount was based on the national average weekly industrial wage, which was $115 in 1968. Heads
of households received larger amounts, based on the number
of dependents. Each dependent, with the exception of the
spouse, received $57.50, which was one-half of the average
weekly wage. The total amount averaged $415.53 per family.
In addition, there was a separate maintenance allowance, if
necessary, for a period of up to four weeks. Costs of storage
and removal of household goods were also covered by an

allowance, and the transportation of the worker and his family
was paid for. In addition, a loan of up to $1,500 was made
available to selected heads of families for the purpose of purchasing a home within 12 months after relocation, and loans
of up to $200 were made available to relocatees for the pur-
chase of a car within six months after relocation. The total
costs of relocation, excluding loans, was $114,843, and the
average grant for all relocatees was $309.59.

The 371 relocatees were sent to three demand areas--
High Point, Charlotte, and Greensboro. Most of them were
employed in the furniture, textiles, and transportation industries. Their wages ranged from a minimum of $1.40 an hour
to a maximum of $4.25 an hour, with the typical wage being
in the range of $1.60 to $1.80 an hour. Table 30 presents a
breakdown of the hourly wages of relocatees.

The characteristics of the relocatees in the third mobility
project were as follows:

1. Fifty percent of those moved lived in some sort of
rent-free arrangement in the home area, usually as a tenant.
This can be considered as one factor which helps to explain
why many relocatees preferred to give up the prospect of
higher wages and more stable employment.

2. The majority of relocatees had nine or more years of
education. About one-fourth had a high school education.
However, as mentioned previously, the quality of elementary
and secondary education in rural areas is considerably lower
than in non-rural areas. Not only are the direct costs of education lower, but the opportunity costs of schooling are also
lower in rural areas, simply because there are poorer employment opportunities in such an area.

3. Most of the relocatees were Negroes from the rural
coastal counties. Forty-five were Indians from western
North Carolina. The average distance moved was 162.6
miles, with a range of 70 to 302 miles. The average age of
the typical relocatee was 22, and 192 out of the 371 relocatees
were married.

The North Carolina Manpower Development Corporation
reported a 50 percent success rate on its relocations, based

TABLE 30

Hourly Wages of 371 Relocatees in
the North Carolina Mobility Project

Hourly Wage	Number of Relocatees
$1.40 - 1.49	16
1.50 - 1.59	22
1.60 - 1.69	162
1.70 - 1.79	63
1.80 - 1.89	14
1.90 - 1.99	4
2.00 - 2.09	65
2.10 - 2.19	8
2.20 - 2.29	12
2.30 and over	5
	371

Source: Final Report of the North Carolina Manpower Development Corporation (formerly North Carolina Fund) (June, 1969),
p. 78.

on the usual 60-day test period. Of the 371 workers who were
relocated during the period that the project was in effect, 187
were no longer in the receiving area after 60 days. Ninety-one
were reported to have returned to the home area. (Some dis-
crepancy exists; the U.S. Department of Labor reports that
59 returned to the home area.) Of the remainder, 22 workers
moved out of the state, 19 moved to another city within the
state, and 12 entered the armed services. Legitimately this
group should not be considered as relocation failures unless
there was a reversion to the unemployed status that most
possessed in the home area. Changing employers can be in-
terpreted as a sign of self-confidence and adjustment to a new
urban situation where the rural relocatee is not dependent
upon a single landlord or employer, but can pick his spots in
looking for more money or a job closer to home. Of those
relocatees who returned home, many did so during the months
of April, May, and June--a time when seasonal employment
is available.

A major problem which perhaps should be apparent occurs
when rural workers with little or no job training are relocated
in areas where employment is available. Many jobs which are
readily accessible to this type of worker are "dead-end" jobs
that offer little advancement in pay or in upward mobility.
From industry's point of view, people are needed to fill these
jobs; therefore, training for unskilled workers is not desired.
In essence, training programs provided by a company are dependent upon its needs: it will train janitors to be mechanics
only if its need for mechanics cannot be met in other ways.
A desirable solution to the problem of "dead-end" employment
is to train potential relocatees while they are still in the supply area or to set up incentives for industry to train unskilled
workers, i.e., tax benefits or subsidies. Pre-relocation
training, in particular, would increase a worker's bargaining
power within a given industry as well as his alternatives
among different industries.

An expectation of higher rates of return on investment in
vocational training and basic education in rural poverty areas
can be based on the assumption that there are no artificial re-
strictions on mobility. Naturally a rural poverty area is by
definition an economically depressed area. Most people who
remain in the area will probably face below-average employment opportunities and miss the high-return potential for

investment in migration to a more prosperous location. Thus, the rate of return to investments in the schooling of those who remain is probably lower than the rate which is obtained by all of the people who receive their schooling in the rural poverty area--including those who later move out.

SUMMARY

The purpose of the North Carolina labor mobility projects was to demonstrate that unemployed persons in economically depressed areas of the state could be relocated and employed in the more heavily industrialized Piedmont section. There were three mobility projects. The first began operations in 1965 under the sponsorship of the North Carolina Fund, and lasted from March, 1965, to February, 1966. A total of 278 workers received relocation assistance to move to such cities as Charlotte and High Point. The success rate, as measured by the number of workers who remained in the demand areas, was low--only 33 percent were in the areas a year after relocation. A majority of those workers who left the demand area returned to the home area. A relocation program, if it is to reduce unemployment significantly, must have as its prime purpose a high rate of stable relocations. However, when complicating factors, such as the movement of unskilled workers, are taken into consideration, the first labor mobility project achieved some success.

The second labor mobility project operated from March, 1966, through September, 1967. A total of 489 workers received relocation assistance. More than 90 percent were non-whites from 30 eastern counties, with the remainder from 12 mountain counties. The unemployment rate in these 42 counties in 1967 was 5.9 percent--a rate which is not excessive by national standards. But agricultural employment in these counties had declined by one-fourth during the period 1962-67, and a shortage of 120,000 jobs was forecast by 1970.

The procedures used in relocation were rather different. Recruitment was made in rural areas by a staff of recruiters who used what can be called the "cold canvass" method--walk up and ask a person if he wants a job in the Piedmont.

Boarding houses were used to provide some sort of housing until the relocatees were able to find their own. However, housing was the biggest single problem in arranging relocations for the North Carolina labor mobility projects. Low-rent housing for Negroes, even in segregated districts, was particularly hard to locate. A variety of supportive services were provided to ease the drastic shift from a long-familiar rural area to a complex urban area with totally different standards and values.

The third labor mobility project provided 371 workers with relocation assistance. The North Carolina Manpower Development Corporation had planned to move 1,000 persons, but the lack of adequate housing proved to be a major deterrent. Approximately one-half of all of the relocatees had left the demand area by the end of the project. This, in itself, cannot be regarded as a failure of relocation, for some workers took employment in other areas of the state or in other states.

APPENDIX C THE MISSISSIPPI
STAR PROJECT

The Mississippi STAR Project involved the relocation of
rural workers from underdeveloped and low-income regions
of the state to other areas within and immediately outside of
the state. In some respects, the project was similar to the
North Carolina project, in that relocations were made to
growth areas within the state. However, the project population may have been a little worse off in terms of income
and employment opportunities. The Mississippi Delta region,
which was one of the supply areas, has long been an agricultural center, dominated by cotton produced mainly by hand
labor. Since 1960, new crops have appeared in the Delta,
and production methods now substitute weed-killing chemicals
for human cotton choppers and mechanical methods for human
cotton pickers. This shift eliminated more than 50,000 agricultural jobs during the period 1960-67. Poverty is endemic
in the region. In 1966, approximately four-fifths of all non-
white families were making less than $3,000 a year.

The relocatees were selected from four areas. The first
area was comprised of Coahoma and Tunica counties, which
are located in the Delta region, in the northwestern part of
the state. These counties are predominantly Negro, and the
majority of relocatees were unskilled Negro laborers from
cotton farms. The second area consisted of the counties of
Alcorn, Benton, Marshall, Pontotoc, Prentiss, Tippah, and
Union, in the northeast highland area of the state. This area
is predominantly white, and most relocatees were unskilled
white laborers and sharecroppers. The third area, in the
southwestern part of the state, was comprised of Adams,
Claiborne, Jefferson, and Warren counties. The population
of these counties is about evenly divided between whites and
Negroes. The majority of relocatees were displaced, unskilled Negro laborers who had depended upon the timber and
lumber industry for employment. The fourth area was composed of Jones and Wayne counties, which are located in the

southeastern part of the state. Relocatees were mostly unskilled Negro laborers, who had depended upon the timber
and lumber industry for employment.

The demand areas to which the relocatees were sent were
linked to the supply areas in terms of geographic propinquity.
Workers from the Delta counties were relocated in Memphis,
and workers from the northeastern counties were relocated
in Tupelo. Other demand areas were Jackson, Hattiesburg,
and Pascagoula. All of the demand areas are industrialized,
and have experienced low levels of unemployment in recent
years. There was a demand for both skilled and unskilled
workers in these areas. Although most relocatees were
placed in unskilled jobs, there were some who possessed the
skill requirements necessary to obtain work in skilled occupations.

One problem which confronts any attempt to relocate the
rural poor is a deficiency in their educational backgrounds.
Mississippi has the lowest per capita income of any state,
and in general, schools outside of the urban areas are poorly
equipped. Illiteracy rates are high in the rural areas, and
the state does not have a mandatory school attendance law.
Along with a low level of educational attainment, there is
also a social dependence on the part of the unemployed poor
upon an employer. Workers are often held in a position of
debt servitude by an employer who wishes to assure himself
of an adequate labor force as seasonal employment demands
occur. There is also an emotional and psychological dependence on the part of the rural poor upon family and friends.

The Mississippi relocation project was the responsibility
of Systematic Training and Redevelopment Incorporated
(STAR). Funding was provided by the Department of Labor
and the Office of Economic Opportunity. Although the primary purpose of the project was to explore the potential of
relocation aid to unemployed rural workers, STAR also provided counseling services to relocatees, basic education, and
vocational training. Considerable emphasis was placed upon
counseling as a component of total assistance to the relocatees. This service was provided by field coordinators in both
the supply and the demand areas. Recruitment was done by
contacting local employment offices and welfare offices, and
by directly contacting potential relocatees in the supply area.

Job placement in the demand area was made by contacting local employment offices, and by making personal calls on business firms.

RELOCATION

Direct financial assistance for relocation was of four types: travel allowances for interviews, travel allowances to take employment, settling-in allowances, and payments for the removal of household goods. The settling-in allowance amounted to $115 for a single relocatee, $115 for a married relocatee plus $115 for his wife, and $57.50 for each child, up to four children. (These are the final rates; the original rates--$75 plus $25 for each family member-- proved to be too low.) The maximum allowance was set at $460. In addition, there was a separate maintenance allowance which was paid if suitable housing could not be found in the demand area. This allowance amounted to $57.50 a week for a period which could not exceed four weeks. The settling-in allowance was spaced in three equal payments to insure that the relocatee would remain on the job for at lease a full month. The first payment was made when the relocatee began work, the second payment was made following his second week on the job, and the final payment was made after the relocatee had worked one full month. The logic for the use of the installment method of payment was based on the fact that the first month is a critical adjustment period for most relocatees.

The Mississippi relocation project extended over a two-year period, 1966-68. A total of 448 workers received relocation assistance at a cost of $105,737--an average of $250 per relocatee. All were unemployed prior to relocation, and their overall average educational level was 8.3 years-- a low level of educational attainment. More than 90 percent had no financial resources prior to relocation. Most relocatees were placed in jobs that required little or no skill--general laborer, warehouse helper, sanitation worker, longshoreman, and plumber's helper. However, some relocatees had sufficient training and education to qualify as welders and machine operators. In general, it can be said that most of the jobs offered little opportunity for future advancement. Although

this must be considered an unfavorable aspect of relocation,
the point has to be made that at least jobs were available for
those who were willing to leave the uncertainty of employment
in the home area.

Table 31 presents data which pertain to the characteristics
of the relocatees who were moved during the 1967-68 period
of operation.

Although nothing definitive can be said about benefit-cost
ratios, there is no reason to expect them to be negative. The
average hourly earnings of all of the relocatees after moving
was $1.71, compared with an average hourly wage of $1.36
prior to moving. It must be remembered, however, that the
average relocatee had been unemployed for 15 weeks prior to
relocation and was not earning anything. In view of this fact,
the potential monetary income gain from relocation is much
higher than is indicated. A reduction in the real income differential can be expected, as was true for the North Carolina
relocation project, because of higher housing costs in the demand areas. In terms of money income, it is likely that all
of the relocatees made less than a poverty-level income of
$3,000 annually, and it is apparent that relocation would en-
able most to earn incomes in excess of this level, provided
they remained employed for a full year.

The rate of return to the home areas must be considered
high. In all of the labor mobility projects, an unsuccessful
relocatee was operationally defined as a person who had been
relocated with financial assistance, but who left the area of
relocation before two months expired. It is conceivable, however, that some persons found employment in other areas,
and so it is difficult to label the relocation as unsuccessful.
Two months is too short a time period to judge a relocation
as successful or unsuccessful; it would be better to use a one-
year period after relocation. If a worker was still employed
in the demand area or in another area, his relocation can be
counted a success. On the other hand, if the worker is unemployed or back in his original status in the home area, the relocation can be considered a failure.

During the first operational period of the project, 115
workers received relocation allowances. After two months,
one-third had left the demand area. The second operational

TABLE 31

Characteristics of Relocatees in the Mississippi STAR Project

Age	Average Weeks Unemployed	Average Educational Level	Average Old Job Hourly Wage	Average New Job Hourly Wage
18 - 27	18.0	10.0	$1.52	$1.68
28 - 37	11.3	9.2	1.58	1.76
38 - 47	17.6	6.9	1.16	1.64
48 - 57	22.1	8.2	1.32	1.93
58 - 72	10.3	7.5	1.23	1.54

Source: Final Report of the Mississippi STAR Project, p. 49.

243

phase of the project provided more extensive counseling and
supportive services. The change from a seasonal work cycle
to a scheduled daily work commitment proved to be a difficult
adjustment for many relocatees. Emotional support had to
be provided by the counselors. A total of 333 workers received relocation assistance, and after two months, 78, or
23 percent, had left the demand area. Judging from the experiences of projects in other states, it is probable that the
rate of return to the home area was much higher after a year.
It can be argued, however, that relocation could be considered
a success even if only 20 percent of the relocatees remained
in the demand areas permanently. Presumably, the entire
cost of relocation would be paid for by the higher earnings
and improved life style of the 20 percent. It is doubtful that
employment opportunities in the home area would offer any
viable alternative to relocation.

Unsuccessful relocations were the highest among young
single workers. This tended to reflect the results for similar projects involving the rural unemployed. The vast majority of the unsuccessful relocatees were unskilled workers,
performing assembly line and general laborer duties. This
points out the need for better education and vocational training
in rural areas. Lack of housing was the most important factor
in causing some relocatees to return to the home area. However, housing costs were not considered to be a problem, as
62 percent of relocatees interviewed in a random sample indicated that housing costs were the same or less in the new
area.

The Mississippi relocation project provides an excellent
example of guided migration. Mississippi is a state which
has been losing population for years, although recently this
trend has been reversed. Most of this population loss can be
attributed to the outmigration of Negroes from the state. This
pattern has been traditionally northward to such cities as
Chicago and St. Louis. In many cases, particularly at first,
when there was a need for unskilled workers in the large
cities, the migration was successful. In recent years it is
more likely than not that migration leads simply to more unemployment in the urban slums. But the Mississippi project
placed workers in available jobs, mostly within the state.
Outside of Memphis, it would be difficult to call any of the
places to which relocatees were sent major cities.

In the process of worker relocation from rural to urban
areas, one factor which has to be considered is the need to
effect a change in the attitude of rural individuals toward
work and toward life in general. In projects involving the relocation of rural workers, efforts had to be made to break
the psychological dependence on the home environment--a
dependence that has been passed down from one generation to
the next. In terms of work experience, a change from a seasonal work cycle to a regular and routine daily work schedule
proved difficult for many rural relocatees. This indicates
that for many relocatees, counseling and other supportive
services may be even more important than the actual relocation.

SUMMARY

Traditionally, Mississippi has been dominated by two
major industries--cotton farming and lumber. Both industries employed large numbers of unskilled and undereducated
workers. In recent years, technological advances in the use
of chemical fertilizers and farm equipment reduced the need
for workers in the cotton fields. Concomitant with these advances were similar technological changes in the lumber and
timber industry, which also led to the displacement of labor.
As a result, the state began efforts to attract industry through
the use of tax concessions and other industrial development
incentives. Many small industries have moved into the state
to take advantage of a relatively cheap labor supply as well
as the tax incentives. However, unemployment and underemployment continue to be a problem, particularly among those
who live in rural areas. Migration northward has been a traditional solution to this problem, but the pattern of migration
has often been misdirected.

The Mississippi STAR projects took workers from rural
areas within the state and placed them in jobs in urban centers
in the state and in Memphis, Tennessee. Most of the workers
were placed in jobs requiring little or no skill, which are
preferable to the alternative of no employment in the home
area. Some direction was also given to migration from rural
to urban areas.

APPENDIX **D** THE NORTHERN
MICHIGAN PROJECTS

The purpose of the Northern Michigan labor mobility projects was to relocate unemployed workers who had received MDTA training in employment in the more industrialized areas of Michigan and Wisconsin. These projects were conducted by Northern Michigan University, which àlso provided the job training in various programs at its Area Training Center. In one respect, the projects were similar to those conducted in West Virginia, in that workers were relocated from a depressed area within the state.

The Upper Peninsula of Michigan has long been a problem area. Although it has an abundance of natural resources, it has experienced a rather high rate of unemployment for a number of years. Seasonal unemployment is a particular problem. The average unemployment rate over the period 1962-67 ranged from a high of 13.3 percent in March to 5.5 percent in September. The average unemployment rate for 1967 was 7.5 percent. This area of Michigan has had little success in attracting industry. The more important market areas are far removed, and transportation facilities are inadequate. Climate and terrain limit agriculture to a minor activity, and the only industry common throughout this area is forestry and its related industries. Tourism provides some seasonal employment. The seasonality of employment in the area is reflected in the fact that one out of every four families has an average income of less than $3,000 a year.

The population from which relocatees were selected consisted of three groups: enrollees in MDTA training programs; workers referred from a basic education and pre-vocational training program which was designed to upgrade the industrial skills of welfare recipients; and workers from the Neighborhood Youth Corps. All groups were to have vocational training prior to relocation. Basic education was also provided, including assistance in family and social adjustment to prepare potential relocatees for employment. The training programs placed emphasis not only on job efficiency but also on

247

dependability, punctuality, and other desirable work habits. Workers were pre-tested by the Michigan Employment Security Commission before being referred to job training.

The Northern Michigan labor mobility projects followed a fairly standard format. Unemployed workers were given some form of job training and were relocated where jobs were available. The primary demand or receiving areas to which the relocatees were sent were the Detroit area in southeastern Michigan and the Milwaukee area in southeastern Wisconsin. Pre-employment interview grants were provided to potential relocatees to help defray expenses incurred in traveling for job interviews. Job placement in most instances was effected through the state employment service within the demand area.

There were three projects which extended over the period 1965-68. The first project operated from April 1 to September 30, 1965, and relocated MDTA trainees who had been enrolled in various training programs at the Area Training Center operated by Northern Michigan University. A total of 108 persons were relocated, and 81 received relocation assistance, which took the form of direct loans. The second labor mobility project began in March, 1966, and extended through June, 1967. The number of workers relocated increased to 306, and the number of persons who received relocation allowances amounted to 273. Grants replaced loans as the financial form of relocation assistance. The third project operated from September, 1967, to September, 1968. Workers relocated totaled 295, and 241 received relocation assistance.

The results of the second project indicate that the monetary gains made by the relocatees after relocation are considerable. The average hourly earnings before relocation of the 273 workers who had received relocation allowances was $1.59. This, of course, was based on earnings when last employed. The average hourly earnings after relocation of the 273 workers was $2.47. The average overall gain per relocatee was approximately $36 a week, or $1,872 a year. [17] These material gains are reduced to some degree by high living costs in the demand areas to which the relocatees were sent. However, the average relocatee could be characterized as a person who changed from either a publicly assisted life or a life in which seasonal employment could be expected.

Relocation assistance included a travel allowance, a separate maintenance allowance if housing could not be found in
the demand area, a settling-in allowance, and an allowance
for the removal of household possessions. Grants were used,
and the total amount expended in the relocation process was
$86,628--an average cost per relocatee of $317. The total
administrative costs involved in moving the 273 relocatees
were $119,020--an average cost of $436 per relocatee. The
average total cost of moving a relocatee was $753, and the
average distance moved per relocation was 313 miles. This
average cost of $750 can be compared with the projected av-
erage overall gain during the first year of relocation of $1,872.
The return on the cost of relocation can be considerable within
a short period of time, provided that the relocatees remain
employed. In addition to the assistance and administrative
costs of relocation, an additional $7,778 was spent on pro-
viding grants to relocatees for pre-employment interviews.
This type of arrangement is desirable, for it increases a
worker's chance for a successful relocation.

This project had some of the prerequisites that would appear to be necessary for the operation of a successful national
program of relocation. The relocatees had received some
form of job training prior to relocation. This training was
for a wide variety of jobs, many of which could not be considered as "dead-end." Of the 273 relocatees who received
relocation assistance, 28 were trained to be draftsmen and
17 were trained to be tax assessors. Other relocatees were
trained as auto mechanics, diesel mechanics, welders, machine tool operators, nurses, refrigerator mechanics, electrical appliance repairmen, and data processors. These
workers were pre-tested by the employment service and given
a job skill. Workers who possessed little skill potential were
"weeded out" before and during training. Supportive services,
including counseling, was provided the relocatees after their
arrival in the demand areas.

In comparison with most of the other labor mobility
projects, the success rate, as measured by the number of
relocatees still in the demand area after two months, was
quite good. A very high number of relocatees, 140 out of 273,
were in the demand area two months after relocation. The
performance of employment in the demand area is the real
test of the success or failure of a relocation project, and the

normal 60-day follow-up after relocation cannot be used to prove conclusively that this test is a success or failure. However, the attrition rate in all of the labor mobility projects is the highest during the first month after relocation. Afterwards, the attrition rate can be projected as from 3 to 4 percent of the remaining relocatees for each month up to a year. This does not mean that all of the relocatees leave the demand area and go elsewhere; it means that the attrition occurs to a point where perhaps a hard core 40 percent of the relocatees remain permanently relocated. Based on the experimental relocation projects, no one can say what the percentage of truly successful relocations is, because no follow-up studies a year or two after relocation have been made.

After the two-month follow-up on relocation, 59 workers were no longer with the initial demand area employer. However, of this total, 11 were inducted into the armed services, and 10 did not report to the job. Seventeen quit to return to the home area and were unemployed, and 12 returned home to accept employment. Several workers had quit the original job to accept other employment in the area of relocation.

The principal and most persistent problem which faced the majority of the relocatees was an inability to secure adequate housing within the demand area. Most relocatees cited housing expenses as the most important problem of relocation. As a general rule, those workers who were relocated in the larger metropolitan areas of Detroit and Milwaukee found the housing situation more critical, in terms of both availability and economy, than those relocating in smaller urban areas. Efforts were made toward the latter stages of the project to find relocation sites where suitable housing could be obtained. Howell, Michigan, a town of 4,500 persons in the Detroit metropolitan area, was selected as one relocation site because it was experiencing a great demand for labor attributable to a heavy influx of industry.

Northern Michigan University's relocation projects revealed that it was almost impossible to obtain jobs for and relocate persons who were unskilled and who lacked motivation to obtain job training. For these persons, it would appear that the only type of employment could be on public works programs financed by the federal government. It is argued by some persons that the federal government should serve as an employer of last resort for those who lack the capability to be assimilated into the regular labor force. This may well prove to be necessary.

Most relocatees were placed in jobs in the satellite areas of Detroit and Milwaukee. The second project placed 54 relocatees in suburban communities of 10,000 or less, and 65 in towns of 50,000 to 100,000. To a certain extent, efforts were made to avoid placing relocatees in areas where the transition from a rural to an urban environment would prove to be difficult.

Is relocation assistance an important factor in increasing a worker's willingness to relocate? This particular question was asked of 253 workers who had received financial assistance in relocating. Eighty-one replied that they would not have moved without it; 60 replied that they would have moved anyway, but relocation assistance permitted an earlier move; 73 said that they might have moved without financial assistance; and 39 indicated that they would have moved anyway, without relocation assistance. For the majority of these workers, relocation assistance was the key factor in inducing a move to another area.

NOTES

1. Data furnished by West Virginia Department of Employment Security.

2. Agricultural Policy Institute, "Estimates of Personal Income in North Carolina by County for 1966" (North Carolina State University, 1969).

3. North Carolina Bureau of Employment Security Research, North Carolina Work Force Estimates (Raleigh, 1968), pp. 1-3.

4. See Martin Schnitzer, "Programs for Relocating Workers Used by Governments of Selected Countries," Joint Economic Committee Monograph, Congress of the United States (Washington, D.C.: Government Printing Office, 1965), p. 52.

5. Ibid., p. 52.

6. For a cost-benefit analysis of the first North Carolina labor mobility project, see Paul R. Johnson, "Labor Mobility: Some Costs and Returns," unpublished report prepared by the United States Department of Labor.

7. "General Economic and Social Characteristics, North Carolina, U.S. Census of Population (1960). The figures need to be updated.

8. Estimates made by the Committee on Manpower and Economic Development, North Carolina Fund, and included in the final report of the North Carolina Mobility Project, pp. 28-30.

9. Ibid., p. 35.

10. Final Report of the North Carolina Fund Mobility Project (November 30, 1967), pp. 48-50.

11. Ibid., p. 51.

12. Charles K. Fairchild, "Rural Disadvantaged Mobility," Labor Law Journal (August, 1969).

13. Ibid., p. 14.

14. Ibid., p. 15.

15. Ibid., p. 20.

16. Ibid., pp. 22-24.

17. Final report of the Northern Michigan labor mobility project for 1966-67.

ABOUT THE AUTHOR

Martin Schnitzer is Professor of Finance in the College of Business Administration at the Virginia Polytechnic Institute. He serves as a consultant to the Joint Economic Committee and the House Ways and Means Committee of the U.S. Congress and as a member of President Nixon's task force on rural development. He also served as a member of President Nixon's task force on public welfare. He is a specialist on European economic policy and has published several monographs for the Joint Economic Committee on this subject. He has also received four research grants for work in Europe.

Professor Schnitzer was formerly the Editor of the Virginia Social Science Journal. He has published a number of articles and books in comparative economic systems and public finance.

Dr. Schnitzer received a Ph.D. in Economics at the University of Florida and has done advanced work in summer institutes at the Harvard Business School and the University of Virginia.